From *The Nation*

"American-type democracy, by turns reeling under Communist invective and waltzing to Chamber of Commerce panegyric, might have gone mad long ago if it did not occasionally make its way out into the bracing air of informed criticism. . . .

"This book of essays . . . is the latest such appraisal, and should be welcomed with enthusiasm. If the content of its criticism leaves this reviewer dissatisfied, that should not diminish the importance of the book, for it touches upon almost every major question asked about democracy in the current debates. And its writers bring high competence to the discussion. . . .

"Read this book. It is stimulating."

—From a review in *The Nation* by Howard Zinn, Chairman of the Department of History and Social Science, Spelman College (Atlanta University)

DEMOCRACY

TODAY

Problems and Prospects

SAMUEL H. BEER
  Harvard University

LEON D. EPSTEIN
  University of Wisconsin

LOUIS HARTZ
  Harvard University

CHARLES E. LINDBLOM
  Yale University

J. ROLAND PENNOCK
  Swarthmore College

Edited by
WILLIAM N. CHAMBERS
ROBERT H. SALISBURY
  Washington University

COLLIER BOOKS
NEW YORK, N.Y.

Democracy Today originally appeared under the title *Democracy in the Mid-Twentieth Century*

This Collier Books edition is published by arrangement with William N. Chambers and Robert H. Salisbury

Collier Books is a division of The Crowell-Collier Publishing Company

First Collier Books Edition 1962

Contents

Foreword

THIS VOLUME IS the product of an investigation of some of the critical issues of our time—the nature, achievements, difficulties, and future of our political way of life.

The investigation began with a Conference on Democracy at Washington University, St. Louis, in May 1958. The essays in this book were first prepared as papers for that Conference, which was sponsored by the University's Department of Political Science. Our meetings, however, included a dozen scholars from various universities in addition to the present authors, and the original papers were substantially revised as a result of the Conference dialogue and of critiques by the editors. They were first published as a series of related essays by Washington University in 1960, under the title *Democracy in the Mid-Twentieth Century*. They appear here with only minor changes, primarily to keep it up to date.

Our gratitude is due to Ethan A. H. Shepley, then Chancellor of the University, who took a serious and effective interest in our desire to further the exploration of democratic problems, and to James S. McDonnell, President of the McDonnell Aircraft Corporation of St. Louis, whose long-standing interest in fundamental public questions led him to support the Conference. All of the participants—and this book —are also indebted to Professor Robert G. McCloskey of Harvard University, who presented an able summary at the concluding session of the Conference in which he identified major lines of research in democratic studies indicated by the papers and the discussion.

Problems of democratic government have concerned thoughtful men for a good many centuries. Faced as we are today by the challenge of rival systems, understanding of such problems becomes even more important. Yet the expansion of reliable knowledge has not so far provided a clarification of the democratic issue adequate to our condition.

The Conference was a discussion in which social scientists sought to bring their best intellectual tools to bear toward such a clarification. The essays as they now stand, commenting as they do on one another and related as they are in the editors' introductory chapter, constitute what we hope will prove a fruitful continuation of the discussion in book form.

Thomas H. Eliot
Professor of Political Science
Washington University

St. Louis, Missouri
February, 1962

Democracy Today

The Democratic Issue: Values and Structures

By William N. Chambers and Robert H. Salisbury
Washington University

THE FIVE CONFRONTATIONS of problems and prospects of democracy in this book constitute a varied and yet cohesive exploration. They raise basic concerns in common, tracing the road democracy has travelled; analyzing its norms, structure, and functioning today; and weighing the future of democratic ideals and democratic systems. They mark new paths by posing critical questions of democracy in theory and practice— questions of essential public as well as scholarly concern. Finally, they point toward concrete research and improved understanding as means to strengthen the functioning of democracy.

The common problems these essays treat were not "given" in advance. Few inquiries in the social sciences begin with full understanding of such questions. Any initial formulation of problems undergoes change as inquiry proceeds, as discussion uncovers new facets of the subject, as implicit premises or new interpretations are explored. In short, not only are the "answers" in an intellectual quest seldom apparent at the outset. In the process of thinking, problems themselves are often redefined.

All of us—the present authors and the participants in the Conference out of which these essays grew—began with the assumption that the issue of democracy itself was subject to question and uncertainty in the Twentieth century. We recognized the ambiguities present in common conceptions of democracy, and the difficulty in relating abstract conceptions to the day-to-day realities of going systems. Instead of seeking abstract agreement as to what democracy is or ought to be, we chose to approach the issue by exploring certain dimensions of democratic ideals and realities. We inquired into fundamental philosophic assumptions of democracy;

into relationships between interest groups, parties, government, and administration in modern democracies; into the impact of economic structure on the democratic polity; into questions of leadership in democracy; and into questions of democratic control in shaping foreign policy. All of these areas seemed obviously important to an understanding of democracy's situation and prospects.

In reviewing these areas, we came gradually to what was perhaps the most significant result of our interchange. This was an emerging conception of *why* we are concerned about democracy, and *what* we might do about our concern. This conception emphasizes aspects of the problem hitherto largely unstated or unexplored.

The essays in this volume all consider this issue. In some measure, however, the whole is greater than the sum of its parts. Our intent here is to suggest some aspects of the total intellectual dialogue which are not entirely apparent in the essays taken individually, but which were significant results of a process of collective thinking.

I

The focal problem stems from an apparent contemporary sense of discrepancy between ideal and practice. More precisely, this involves a perception of a gap between an exalted picture of democracy we inherit from our Western tradition on the one hand, and the reality of democracy as we see it today on the other.

Thus Louis Hartz finds us bound by a classical "image" of democracy. It is an individualistic, equalitarian image of direct popular control through rational agreement and action —an ideal derived from revolutionary-democratic thinkers like Locke and Rousseau, or from the Jeffersonian dream. This image was a powerful weapon in democracy's attack on feudalism and monarchy, with their rigidities, irrationalism, and inequalities. Today, however, democracy's historical ties to class interest and its own irrationalisms are exposed, its concentrated power in massive corporations and group associations is laid bare, its group conflict is apparent, and it portent of new elites is loudly proclaimed. We find ourselves dismayed because actual democracy in mass societies cannot fulfill the promises of the pristine image. As a result we experience pessimism, a kind of "psychological funk" about the workings and prospects of actual democracy. This is particularly so when we face the contest for uncommitted minds against world Communism, with its revolutionary *élan* and utopian promises.

The answer, Mr. Hartz argues, is not in boot-strap efforts to recapture the *élan* of democracy's own revolutionary infancy. It is not in cries for new democratic prophets to provide re-evocations of the old democratic faith. The "apocalyptic purism" of any vision of a new system is inevitably disappointed as that system evolves into a going concern. It cannot regain its utopian enthusiasm by artificial respiration or inspired rhetoric. Our hope lies rather in an informed understanding of the operating necessities of democracy under modern conditions. It requires "frank and unfrightened recognition" of contemporary democratic reality with its shortcomings as well as its virtues. Furthermore, Communism has over-promised even more than democracy, and much of the ideological conflict between the two may be resolved in "a kind of reverse competition in the process of disillusionment." Thus we may gain if we replace our impossible Eighteenth century image and its resulting disillusionment with Twentieth century conceptions of democracy as a useful functioning system. We need an "un-illusioned" acceptance of democracy as a viable reality.

Such acceptance need not entail Panglossian deception. Democracy today certainly faces problems other than diminished faith in itself, diminished sense of purpose. Several which touch the heart of democracy as a living system and thus recur again and again throughout these essays may be noted here. Group association is inevitable and functionally valuable in modern society; but groups may exercise coercion over their members which threatens their individuality. A degree of shared outlook, of conformity, is essential if democracy is to work; but there is danger in the potentiality of a mass mind attuned to the mass media—and each week's supply of these media provides instances of trivialization, of inflation of some issues and under-playing of others, or of distortion. Men must act together to achieve their goals; but modern techniques enlarge the potentialities of mass manipulation at the expense of free, rational choice in thought and action. These are intricate problems, and we need more research and understanding to make our way intelligently among them. Generally, however, the contributors to this volume are optimistic that we have the human resilience to meet them.

The diagnosis that the source of our anxiety about democracy lies in a sense of discrepancy between image and reality underlies or affects all of the essays in this volume. If we cannot put the wine of new *élan* into the bottle of old images, what are we to do? In large measure, the four essays which follow the initial statement of the problem address themselves to two tasks. First, they explore the possibilities of more acceptable images or realistic models of democracy. Second, they examine various aspects of democratic reality in the United States and Great Britain in the light of such new statements of democratic values or norms.

The effort to articulate a more satisfactory concept of democratic values is difficult. Disillusioned with the classical metaphor, we still appear to want or need some shorthand (though poetic or evocative) statement which, in reasonable accord with the facts, justifies and explains our way of doing things, which gives us some sense of direction. We fear that the system does not function the way it should, but we really cannot tell unless we have criteria by which to judge. Is efficiency in solving social problems an essential ingredient in modern democracy, as Samuel H. Beer suggests, and is the British system superior to the American system in such efficiency? It may be argued either that this is not the case, or that some loss in efficiency is a fair price to pay for values more central to democracy. There is room for lively dispute as to whether the nature and impact of the modern market economy and corporate structure, as Charles E. Lindblom outlines it, advances or retards realization of democratic values. Is manipulation of opinion and mass action approaching a point of critical danger to democracy, and how do we determine the danger-point? How much individuality, and how much conformity, is necessary for the operation of democracy, and is the balance today more or less favorable to a healthy democracy than it was in the past? Is concentrated, "big" leadership inherently dangerous to democracy, or is the dispersed, "little" leadership J. Roland Pennock advocates a threat to effective democratic functioning or to the strength of democracies in world politics? Is "big," even elitist leadership essential in foreign policy matters—a question Leon D. Epstein weighs—and, if so, essential there only, or in other areas as well? Is group conflict—especially party conflict—vital to democracy, but at the same time dangerous to a continuity of policy necessary for democratic survival in a threatening world?

Questions like these can hardly be answered by recalling Locke, Rousseau, or Jefferson. Some modern restatement is necessary if we are to clarify the standards we call democratic. Such reformulation is a prerequisite to any informed judgment as to whether particular structures or processes promote or hinder democracy.

Perhaps in the long run democracy may find itself less imperilled than Communism by discrepancies between ideal and fulfillment. The world issue, however, may be won or lost not so much in the long run as in immediate engagements, including the ideological; in which case the question of some reinvigoration of democratic faith or ideology may again be argued as pressing. We may not have time to wait upon the process of disillusionment in the Communist orbit. Thus, the question of reformulating democratic ideas involves not only our own sense of well-being, but the outcome of the confrontation of democracy and Communism in world politics. Ideally, a restatement would inspire unembarrassed commitment in the West, and at the same time delineate a persuasive alternative to Communism in the eyes of the new nations of the world.

II

The essays in this volume contribute in various ways to a democratic restatement. They may be thought of as doing so along two mainstreams of approach. One derives from fairly traditional democratic thought; the other from exploring new conceptions or possibilities latent in Twentieth century developments. The first approach, which borrows much from Mr. Hartz's "classical image" and is stressed in Mr. Pennock's emphasis on "dispersed leadership," focusses on the value of *individual self-realization and free participation*. Without assuming that the individual is a wholly rational being, free from group, class, or mass identifications or influences, it may still be argued that the basic value of democracy is that every person be given the fullest opportunity to fulfill his individual potentialities. The system must function so as to maximize this value, and is justified to the extent that it does so.

The question then becomes, what structures and processes best promote self-realization? In Mr. Pennock's view, the answer lies in a pluralistic society in which power is fragmented, the group structure is complex and diffuse, and many opportunities are given for political participation and for leadership. He suggests that individuality is manifested in vital ways through the performance of leadership functions. In his treatment of leadership, which may be taken as an outline of democratic values as a whole, he contrasts (unrealistic) "extreme" conceptions of democracy and "extreme" conceptions of "autocracy." In the former, decisions would be arrived at by free and equal cooperation in a process of "voluntarism," while in the latter one ruler or a few would exercise domination over all. Democratic actuality today must fall somewhere between these extreme poles, with emphasis on maximizing cooperation and voluntary consent, and on minimizing domination or elitist control. Thus "self-development" may be realized along with "rational adjustment of conflicting interests willingly accepted." However, both conflict and cooperation must be viewed, in contemporary reality, as occurring not so much among the atomistic individuals of the classical model as among a plurality of groups in an ineradicably multi-group society. Actual democracy, then, entails broad dispersion of power and leadership in this pluralism of groups. Emphasis should be on "little" leadership throughout the society in its various groups, and on "dispersed, partly independent decisions," rather than on "central direction." Such diffused leadership and participation is the nearest democratic reality should be expected to come to the classical image. It is also, in itself, a practical application of the democratic, humanistic value of individual self-fulfillment.

Other essays concern themselves with related questions. In particular, Mr. Lindblom considers possible dangers to individual self-realization in manipulation of opinion by advertising and public relations, in "human-relations" engineering, and in the almost neo-feudal arrangements of the modern corporation. Much uncertainty, however, surrounds these points. We really know very little about the effects of opinion manipulation. Is individuality necessarily constricted in a corporate society, or do material affluence and the greater range of choices which leisure and wealth offer, result in an increase in self-realization? Furthermore, Mr. Pennock himself regretfully points out that in many areas of decision-making we have little option. We must accept a large measure of "big" leadership, centralized decision-making, and concentrated power in order to cope with the problems of the economy, society, and world. A system must "first of all be able to govern," and then achieve "such degree of democracy as is compatible with governing well." Does this mean, then, that democracy is dead, or at least sadly debilitated?

What it may mean is that an image of democracy as maximum self-realization is inadequate. Perhaps the basic values and norms of democracy cannot be postulated so heavily in terms of self-realization, and still come into reasonable conformity with Twentieth century reality. In the face of this possible inadequacy, an alternative is most clearly and fully articulated by Mr. Beer in a comparative analysis of British and American democracy. He offers, in what constitutes the discussion's second line of approach to a viable conception of democracy, the key value of *efficiency, or coherence and innovation*. The suggestion here is that a democratic system may be judged, in part at least, by the degree to which it meets these criteria.

This possible new image of democracy is derived largely from observation of developments in Great Britain, particularly since World War II. Its evolution as an advanced industrial society has brought Great Britain to what Mr. Beer calls "collectivist democracy." He suggests that many developments which are particularly notable there apply, or will come to apply, to all Western democracies. "Collectivist" is used, not to denote policies of the welfare state or of over-all economic control, but to describe a high degree of organization in and integration among interest groups, political parties, and government. Contrary to common assumptions in the United States about British politics, *both* pressure groups and parties are "strong," and firmly rooted in vocational groupings. Parties compete for popular and Parliamentary majorities in order to control a government of broad powers. Interest groups do not pursue their goals by efforts to develop a natural consensus of rational, atomistic free wills in opinion and action, as the classical image or much Nineteenth century practice would have it. Rather they work through the great parties and their programs, and particularly rely on "direct and continuous contact" in critical administrative decisions. The executive branch of government in turn depends on party majorities, and consults or negotiates with pressure groups, informally or in formal advisory bodies established by law. Thus parties, group associations, and government are all integrated in a "massive concentration of power." It is this integration and concentration, Mr. Beer maintains, which makes the British system superior to the American system in efficiency. He suggests two aspects of efficiency. One is coherence, or adaptation of means to ends in policy decisions so that given policies are not only consistent but "mutually supporting." Another is innovation, or the capacity in a system to produce solutions to new problems in accord with basic purposes, the capacity "to adapt, to be flexible, to move swiftly and creatively."

Obviously, collectivist developments in the British pattern are not without their dangers. Some cost in lessened individuality immediately comes to mind. Yet the individual personality is by no means submerged in British life, Mr. Beer maintains, and a strong though qualified underlying individualism is retained. Danger may lie in tendencies toward "managerialism" in parties and interest groups, toward bargaining between pressure groups and administrative agencies as *the* mode of arriving at major policy, and toward manipulation of public opinion, especially through party propaganda. However, Mr. Beer discovers substantial democratic life in individual participation *within* parties and other organizations in Great Britain, and in the voter's choice *between* parties in elections. One might add that a system which promotes "firm party majorities," in the electorate and the legislature, rather than the *ad hoc* majorities from issue to issue so frequent in American politics, may lay claim not only to efficiency, but to democracy buttressed by efficiency.

Quite aside from such possible dangers, Mr. Lindblom and Mr. Pennock in effect reject Mr. Beer's model as such. They not only offer an image of democracy more in accord with American practice as serving best the central value of human dignity, and argue that some loss of efficiency may be well worth the democratic candle. They also see American pluralism, with its decentralization or dispersed leadership, as a viable model, one which *works,* and is not necessarily less efficient, innovative, or coherent than British concentration. Indeed, Mr. Lindblom argues that a substantially decentralized decision-making system, without central overview or coordination and without "collectivist bargaining" among concentrated units of power, may prove superior in achieving efficiency of performance. He cites the price system in a market economy to support the hypothesis that a system of fragmented power can achieve impressive innovation and substantial coherence of policy. He suggests a number of useful parallels between a market economy and a decentralized polity.

Dealing with the special case of foreign policy, Mr. Epstein goes part way with Mr. Beer, emphasizing the inevitability of considerable centralization in decision-making. However, he specifically disagrees about the kind of party structure most likely to produce coherence in policy. A system of strong, integrated parties may eventuate in *in*coherence in governmental policy when there are changes of the party in power. Foreign policy consensus, and policy coherence and flexibility—insofar as they depend upon support in the whole society—may be impeded by centralized bargaining. Collectivist structures and practices may result in a rigidified pattern of interest representation and intensified policy conflict. Instead, Mr. Epstein elaborates the concept of the attentive public—a necessarily select though not exclusive grouping composed of those who are interested in and informed about foreign affairs. He suggests that debate frequently can and does take place in or before this public, affording a limited but significant measure of popular control over centralized leadership. When the attentive public performs this function, it constitutes a kind of "elitist democracy," comparable perhaps to Nineteenth century Britain, in which the "people" as a whole generally remain passive elements in the policy-making process. Nevertheless, this may be a realistic revision of democratic norms.

Even limited participation by the "go-to-meeting minority" does not always function effectively, as Mr. Epstein notes. Leaders may manipulate or ignore opinion, even the opinion of the informed elite. Moreover, serious, prolonged conflict within the attentive public might threaten the continuity of policy. The attentive public usually is relatively unstructured, however, and its influence is brought to bear through individuals and *ad hoc* groups rather than through disciplined parties. It functions in both Great Britain and the United States in a context of substantial consensus concerning foreign policy objectives, and such wide areas of agreement assure considerable coherence and continuity of policy. Innovation and democratic participation are provided through criticisms at the margins of policy emanating from the attentive public. Thus, at least for the issues of foreign policy, Mr. Epstein offers a description of a part of the functioning reality which may also serve as a sophisticated model for a viable democracy.

The two broad images of democracy developed in these essays are not mutually exclusive, but neither are they inevitably correlated. Efficiency is "macrocosmic." It takes an over-all view of the polity and what it ought to "produce," through whatever structures may serve this purpose best. Faith that maximum individual self-realization will promote efficiency in the polity may be justified, Mr. Lindblom argues in effect, by analogy to the price system. On the other hand, Mr. Beer's position cannot be disregarded. The difficulty is that we know little of what results may be anticipated from one way of doing things as compared with another. Thus even if we successfully reformulate a democratic image or model, we will still need to know far more in the way of facts before we can move wisely to implement the goals of the model in practice.

The idea of individual self-realization is "microcosmic," It postulates a norm for individuals, not aggregates. Efficiency in a system may not mean adequate self-realization for its citizens. Do the circumstances of the Twentieth century make it possible to realize both microcosmic or "individual" values, and macrocosmic or "societal" values? Again, there is little clarity about the question, or about the structures which are appropriate for putting the values into practice, because we lack so much of the necessary data. Is a decentralized structure essential to individual self-realization? or are the social and economic security and well-being which are prerequisites for self-realization more likely to be provided and protected in a centralized democratic system? Plausible cases may be made for both alternatives. Without surer knowledge and understanding, however, we cannot be certain that either or both might not betray us.

III

Such considerations raise the problem of continuing, focussed democratic studies, of basic and applied research.

The very theses of the essays themselves, based on scholarly competence as they are, suggest further inquiry; and of course, the writers suggest specific lines of research. Most broadly, we might ask—is the pessimism, the psychological funk about the operation of democracy today which Mr. Hartz postulates, a feeling widely spread among ordinary citizens in western democracies? and if so, what of the shape, intensity, and nuances of such feelings? Has Great Britain moved as far, and the United States so little, toward collectivist democracy as Mr. Beer contends? and if so, are the values of efficiency as fully realized in collectivists practices as he suggests, and what, in detail, are the current or potential costs? Are the pluralistic, dispersed-leadership conceptions of American democratic functioning Mr. Lindblom and Mr. Pennock offer wholly accurate and comprehensive representations of contemporary

American reality? What, in concrete cases, are the processes of foreign policy formulation Mr. Epstein treats? what individuals and what groups are involved, and what relative weight, power, or influence do they command?

Five discrete, recurring research questions which emerged in the original discussion were summarized by Robert G. McCloskey. Two of the five may be thought of as being particularly relevant to any image of democracy as individual self-realization and participation. These are—

Manipulability. This involves questions as to whether and to what extent people can be and are manipulated in politics, and what constitutes manipulation. It also raises the questions of how much manipulation is compatible with norms of self-realization, and how much may be required for democratic functioning under modern conditions. These latter questions depend on further clarification of our conceptions of democracy and democratic standards, but not much can be said about them until we know more about manipulation in empirical fact.

Individuality. In modern societies, in political systems we call democratic, how much opportunity actually exists for individual decision-making? If such opportunities are actually greater in Twentieth century, complex societies than they were in earlier centuries, do such opportunities lead to individuality in decisions in practice, or to withdrawal, "escape from freedom," purposelessness, alienation? What degree of individuation or individual decision-making is desirable or possible in contemporary society and political democracy?

Two other research questions may be thought of as being particularly relevant to, or refocusing the issue of, conceptions of democracy in terms of efficiency, taken as coherence and innovation.

The Self-Regulating Polity. Is a political system analogous to the market-economy or based on patterns of widely dispersed leadership viable under modern conditions, workable as an answer to contemporary problems? Can it provide a sense of direction or purpose, as well as efficiency? Self-regulating polities have been proposed as useful models of both democratic norms and efficiency, and yet it has been suggested that modern industrial societies may inevitably evolve toward a kind of "collectivist democracy." The empirical and normative aspects of such contentions must be further explored, particularly in connection with questions of effectiveness, leadership, elites or elitism, and so on.

The Collectivist-Democratic Polity. Such a structure has been offered as being very nearly synonymous with democratic efficiency, or coherence and innovation. Yet these concepts require attention to make them clearer and more useful as operational terms. Furthermore, important questions of empirical knowledge arise. How, empirically, do you determine or measure the extent to which one system is more coherent and innovative than another? Is the structure of a system a sufficient guide to an answer, or must other, more subtle matters of attitude and practice also be given considerable attention?

A final particular research question would appear to be equally relevant either to a self-realization image or to an efficiency image of democracy—

The Special Policy Area. Foreign policy and major domestic crises seem to present special problems in democracy, however construed, as contrasted with elite control. Foreign policy, because of the complexity, need for continuity, and remoteness from popular concern or understanding involved, is often treated as "different," as *the* special policy area. Yet we are not sure in fact that there are major differences in the nature of popular control over foreign as contrasted with much domestic policy-making. What are the facts in these two areas? Given the data, what are desirable norms, in the face of Twentieth century problems and how might these affect the values of democracy?

These and related questions of inquiry do not in themselves constitute a complete, ordered agenda of democratic studies, nor do they exhaust possible research concerns. They do, however, point to areas of uncertainty which suggest further rigorous exploration, if we are to understand democratic functioning better, sustain a healthy democratic way of life, and improve its operation.

Democracy: Image and Reality

By Louis Hartz
Harvard University

THE SYSTEM OF democracy works by virtue of certain processes which its theory never describes, to which, indeed, its theory is actually hostile. But we identify the system with the theory, as if we actually lived by the ancient Jeffersonian image of democracy we cherish, so that when we are confronted with some of the practices which make democracy work we become terrified that the system is breaking up. In large measure the internal "crisis of democracy," heralded since the age of E. L. Godkin, is of this fantastic sort, an agony of the mind rather than of the real world. We have been in the position of the Victorian who, discovering sex, feels that the human race is about to vanish. Biologically this reaction is fantastic, but psychologically there is plenty of evidence to prove that it exists.

Democracy has always worked through group coercion, crowd psychology, and economic power, yet for fifty years these factors have sent a tremor through democratic hearts. It would be absurd, of course, to argue that none of these factors poses a problem for the democratic process. Quite obviously they all do. The tyranny of party and group, if carried beyond a certain point, can begin to nullify the decision of an electorate. Mass opinion, if it reaches a point where it is completely manipulable by a monopolistic force, will also make a sham of the democratic system. And a powerful economic minority clearly has certain bounds within which it must function if democracy is to retain its meaning. But it is one thing to define these problems as problems of "excess," of the necessary machinery of the democratic world somehow getting out of hand, and it is quite another to define them as an apocalyptic "exposure" of democratic institutions. They do indeed expose our theory, which has room for none of them, but they do not expose the real processes by which democracy has always worked.

What I am suggesting, then, is that during the last half century, with respect to domestic factors, we have had a surplus of pessimistic excitement about the "fate of democratic institutions," and that this in turn derives from the discovery of things which challenge the *image* of democracy much more than they do its *practice*. But how does such a situation come about? How can it happen that the theory of a system will leave out so much of the real machinery by which it lives? And why should men so confuse the theory with the machinery that they are led in the end to suffer unreal anxieties?

I

These questions drive us back to the larger issue of the historic development of political systems, and they lead us finally to a new problem facing democracy on the world plane which is more subtle and difficult than any discovered by the familiar theorists of domestic pessimism.

The truth is, no modern political system as it has risen to power has ever developed an image which corresponds to the real procedures by which it works. Nor has this been due to any trick, any conscious hypocrisy of mind. It has been due to the inevitable perspectives of political controversy, which compel a system to define itself in terms of the one it seeks to determine. Its image of itself is a negation of what it seeks to destroy. Thus Marxism, instead of being a picture of socialist society, the nature of which we are only now beginning to discover, is a negative picture of capitalism. And in the same sense the doctrine of liberal democracy, instead of being a description of democratic life, is a negative description of life in the old European world that democracy destroyed. Locke, Rousseau, and Bentham are in this sense not "theorists of democracy" at all: they are the inverted theorists of the "corporate society" of the Seventeenth and Eighteenth centuries.

Once we go back to that society, it is clear enough why

the democratic image these men gave us should be hostile to half of the machinery that was later invented in order to make democracy work. The points at which they assailed the old corporate system were precisely the points at which that machinery was destined to appear: this is one of the crucial correlations involved in our whole problem, the link between the institutions of the corporate world that the classical thinkers denounced and the new inventions of the democratic age that they did not bother to mention. Seeking to emancipate men from the rigid pluralism of church, guild, and province, those thinkers were bound to be "individualists." How could they say, even if they understood the fact, that democracy itself would function through a new pluralism of associations, parties, and groups? Anxious to shatter the claims of revelation, to dissolve the hierarchies based on the notion of mass incompetence, they were bound to be "rationalists." Could they say also that the electorate of a large state, if only to unify itself sufficiently to function, would have to forge a common opinion largely through the use of stereotypes and symbols, and that herein would lie the possibilities of manipulation? Nor is the issue less clear with respect to economic power. The men who gave us our image of democracy were associated with the rise of the middle class, and where there has been no such class democracy has had its difficulties. But seeking to shatter the rule of another older class they could not fail to be universalists, to form an image of pure "equality."

Thus Locke, Bentham, and Jefferson were bound to coin clichés which contradicted half of the institutional reality which has made them triumph in the modern world. The bond between the old institutions of the corporate age and the new institutions of the democratic age, a bond of group pluralism, mass emotion, and elite rule, had, in the nature of things, to remain as hidden as possible. This does not mean, of course, that democracy is really the same as the dying feudalism of the Seventeenth and Eighteenth centuries, that no progress in the direction of individualism, real popular decision, and the equal state has actually taken place. The English worker today has much more of all of these things than he had in the earlier era. But he has them precisely because he is related to a party machine that Locke never described, involved with mass media that Bentham does not mention, the heir of a bourgeois development that finds no place in the "state" of such a late Nineteenth century liberal as T. H. Green. So that what happens in the case of an ascendant social and political system is that it strikes in fact some middle ground between the blazing negative ideals of its origin and the operational necessities of actual life. As a living thing it turns out to be a mad anomaly, a set of ideals half realized through institutions which contradict them, which no one has ever described. And it is always productive, at a certain stage in its later history, of a crowd of thinkers who suddenly discover that no one has ever described it. This is the age of "realism," which mixes with new anxiety a vast amount of empirical research.

But why should the facts be so hard to face? Why, if we see ourselves as we have always been, should we feel that our existence is suddenly threatened? There is really nothing mysterious about this, nothing excessively subtle. We have projected onto the real world the moral difficulties we have actually experienced in perceiving the realities of democratic life. Surely no one will deny that, since the first World War when Walter Lippmann nearly gave up hope for public opinion, we have sustained a considerable shock. The mood of the "muckraker" has become a permanent aspect of our lives, shifting from party machines to the mass media to social or "power elites," forever refueling our Victorian sense of impending doom. And yet it would be a mistake to assume that our anxieties have derived wholly from this false mechanism. Many of the modern "exposures" of democracy have come from Fascism and Communism, or have at least been seconded by them. These ideologies have represented external threats to Western democracy of a most real kind, backed up by guns and bombs, by the territorial power of opposing nations. There has been nothing imaginary about these challenges to our survival. So that what has happened is that the fantastic has somehow gained strength from the real, the fear of "elites" from the fear of

Hitler's bombs. There is a type of emotional rationality which can argue as follows: "How can we deny the Communist exposure of democracy? After all Communism has conquered half the world."

So far I have spoken of our mood of anxiety and realism as if it were itself detached from the empirical world—a response to that world, as horror is the Victorian response to sex, but not a participant in it. Actually, of course, this is far from being true. On the world plane, especially, where democracy meets Fascism and Communism, our current mood has great operational relevance. For these ideologies are utopian, have behind them the driving negative images that democracy had in the day of its origin out of the feudal order. Strictly speaking this was not true of Fascism. Negative it was, a revolt against the whole Enlightenment complex which produced both democracy and Communism, but negative it remained until the end. Communism, however, is a different matter. Rooted itself in the Enlightenment, its battle against capitalism has produced even more vivid promises of emancipation than those produced by democracy in its struggle against the old corporate order: statelessness, abundance, the end of all natural coercion. And there is a sense in which the modern democrat, when he confronts the Communist, is half struck with an image of his earlier, driving, utopian self. But how, in the age of his unillusionment, is he to argue with the Communist? How, burdened with the sadness of self-knowledge, is he to compete with him for the uncommitted world?

This question has given a new dimension to our sense of "crisis," and in the response which it has yielded, has dramatized pathetically the whole development I have been discussing. We have told ourselves again and again that we must "recapture the revolutionary spirit," that we must somehow flog ourselves backward into the halcyon and simplistic age of Paine and Jefferson. But this recommendation, which appears in so many of our political speeches and Chamber of Commerce utterances, we have never been able to follow. It has been the secular analogue to the plea for a religious revival, a political rather than a clerical fideism, and it has suffered the same major disappointments. We should be able to minimize the anxieties which have come from our realism; but the realism itself, for good or for bad, is as irrevocable as the spirit of science in the modern world. In the Twentieth century democracy will never yield another Locke to belabor the claims of the Soviet Union.

But this ought not to leave us with a sense of gloom, the feeling that all is lost. There is another aspect to this situation in which the modern democrat can take a kind of ironic satisfaction. Communism is itself subject to the same process of disenchantment that democracy has experienced, the same principle of rising realism, the same crisis of anxiety. And because its negative ideals are in fact broader than those of democracy, and in certain areas its institutions are a more glaring contradiction of them, its shock of disenchantment is bound to be even more severe than any we have sustained. Have we not already seen this process at work in Communism, from the Western "God That Failed" to the "New Class" of Milovan Djilas? There is mounting evidence to prove that Communism is susceptible to an even more frightful version of the unillusionment we have experienced, the hidden anticlimax which the Enlightenment imposes on all of its children.[1]

I do not mean to say that the Soviet Union will collapse because of the cynicism of its inhabitants, however great the proof of that cynicism may be. Systems work, despite the anguish men have when they discover how they work. But I do mean to say that in the argument with Communism we have more to hope from an inexorable disenchantment on its part than from an impossible attempt to recapture the Eighteenth century on our part. Indeed to repeat with a manufactured passion the simplisms we have outgrown is merely to multiply the anxieties they ultimately generate, and to prolong into the era of Communism's disenchantment the problem of our own. Today democracy has nothing to lose, and everything to gain, from a frank and unfrightened recognition of itself.

II

Let us examine more closely the cycle of negative idealism, middle ground achievement, and ultimate anxiety in the democratic case. I have said that the crucial thing here is the linkage between the institutions of the old corporate order that the classical theorists denounced, and the inventions of the democratic order which for that reason they could not mention. It is a set of strategic links: between the established church and the political party, between the guild and the pressure group, between the ritual symbolism of monarchy and the ritual symbolism of democracy, between the power of the aristocracy and the power of the middle class. Even now certain of these connections seem outlandish, so deeply buried has the strategy of the democratic argument been even in our scholarship on the subject. But it is a pity that these connections have not been more widely stressed, for if they give to Locke, Rousseau, and Bentham a certain devious touch, they at any rate save these men from the charge of massive empirical stupidity. It is bad enough to have to come to terms with an institutional underworld that our ancestors never mentioned, but it is even worse to feel that the problem was produced entirely by their wanton lack of perception.

If we think of the "philosophers of democracy" as the "philosophers of the old corporate order" instead, their radical atomism, their antagonism to the whole rich growth of group pluralism by which democracy works, becomes a practical necessity. It was not merely the fact that the individual in the old order was associated with the hierarchy of church, class, and guild: his whole personality, apart from an ultimate Christian individualism, was defined in terms of them. Nor was this entirely a matter of "coercion," of the restrictions on the liberty of social and territorial movement that the liberal writers stressed so much. There was, as Mr. Penfield Roberts has said, a kind of "social security" principle implicit in the behaviour of the ancient groups, which inspired the individual to look to them for the essential elements of his survival. To cut through the complex reciprocal relationships which bound the individual to the old corporation was thus an adventure in the very discovery of the individual mind, and this in large measure is the meaning of the "state-of-nature" image. We ask: did the classical theorists take that image literally? But whether they did or not, no polemical instrument less powerful could have shaken the rigidities of the group structure they confronted. You needed an explosive individualism in order to create the "individualism" of the democratic myth.

Here, indeed, passion ran so high that our theoreticians could not always retain even a strategic silence with respect to the groups that might emerge in the world they were building. We often find explicit warnings against them, and every graduate student in political theory knows Hobbes' argument for the subjection of corporations to the sovereign in the body politic. If in Locke lesser groups are for the most part damned by omission, they arise again in Rousseau as objects of an explicit fury, the reflection of his bitter hatred of the rigid corporatism of the French Eighteenth century. These smaller "general wills," which might in our own time include the Democratic Party rather than the Catholic Church, the AFL-CIO rather than the local guild, challenged improperly the will of the community as a whole. Nor can the modern realist derive much satisfaction from the famous qualifying phrase of Rousseau, in which he says that if there are going to be lesser general wills one ought to have as many as possible for the purpose of balancing them off against each other. This is not the wisdom of Twentieth century multi-group theorists like Arthur F. Bentley, Earl Latham, or David B. Truman. It is the sadness of a man who, endowed with greater empirical courage than his contemporaries, is trying to reconcile himself to a situation he does not like.

But the concept of the "general will" shows us that there is more involved in our hatred of our own pluralism than our faith in the free individual. Once the great medieval chain of social being was dissolved, once men were emancipated from the fixities of place and class, it was necessary to make sure that they would arrive at a common decision. And in a world of individuals as isolated from one another as those to be found in Locke's state of nature, this was accomplished, for a variety of reasons, by the premise of a moral universalism to which these individuals by virtue of their "right reason" were inexorably chained. On this count it makes no difference whether we speak of "natural law" or the "general will:" in either case we speak of a unity of decision arising out of an absolute which every individual carries in his own heart. The competition of groups, cliques, machines, and parties must always be at war with this absolute, since it implies, if a decision is to be generated by it, the classic relativity of the bargaining process. At worst it implies that political results are achieved through the negotiated antagonisms of sheer power, and at best it implies that they are achieved through the exhaustion which comes after a struggle of competing points of view. In either case the men who participate in this process, if they share as they have the democratic image of the West, are forever on leave from Sunday School. The Jeffersonian purist, John Taylor, one of the most virulent of campaigners, once denounced the American party system because "truth is a thing, not of divisibility into conflicting parts, but of unity."[2]

The distinction between feudal pluralism and democratic pluralism is of course a great one, and it is a measure of the undisciplined nature of symbolism that the negation of the one should provide us with a conscience, an "individualism" and a "general will," which is terrified at the sight of the other. The pluralism of a democratic society has, to begin with, a fluidity unmatched in the older world. After all account is taken of the mobility possible in the Eighteenth century, and the restrictions on social movement in the Twentieth, there can be no question that the range of group choice open to the average individual has been radically enhanced. His "individualism," if it is implemented through the interstices of a thousand groups rather than on the flat terrain of a state of nature, is nonetheless a real thing. In work, in religion, in class, he realizes his freedom to such a degree that Eric Fromm and others have feared that his burden of individual choice in the modern world, in contrast to the earlier time, may be in fact excessive. Nor have the political associations of the Western democracies, for all of the rigidities they may contain, failed to implement the popular will whose symbolism forever denounces them. Here the contrast is stark and unarguable: none of the groups of the feudal or old corporate order, whether one thinks of the church or the province or the guild, were organized for the purpose of mobilizing a popular electorate. They were institutions which did far more to keep the individual "in his place," than they did to implement his opinion in public life. What is thus involved, when our Eighteenth century conscience frightens us of the pluralism we have built, is an acute case of reasoning by false analogy.

There is no need to overdo this point, or to minimize the degree to which in our time associations have grown powerful in the democratic state. There is a sense in which we are forever refighting the struggle against feudal corporatism, and forever taking as our point of departure the images of Locke and Rousseau in the process. When we regulate corporate monopoly, when we limit the coercive power of a labor union, when we control the practices of political parties, the state is protecting the individual from excessive impact of the group and the public from the excessive impact of private power. But this range of policy, which reaches from the Sherman Anti-Trust Act of 1890 to the Taft-Hartley Act of 1947, is governed by a wholly different mood from the one involved in the stern demands of the democratic conscience. It is a question of degree, of drawing the line here rather than there, and has little in common with the apocalyptic purism of the "general will." It represents an implicit recognition that power is distributed over a multitude of centers within the society. And if it does not go so far as the English pluralists of the early Twentieth century, men like John Neville Figgis and Harold J. Laski who actually replaced the state with the group, it does recognize that in the real world of democracy the group is a permanent fact.

There is of course another world in which the "general will" can be realized, and that is the world of dictatorship. We might accuse the early democratic publicists of betraying their own images, for there was not one of them, of course, who was not associated with a pressure group or a faction. But they could easily reject this criticism. They could argue, as John Taylor did, that they were organizing not for the purpose of creating a continuous pluralism but for the purpose of finally emancipating a popular will which would function thereafter according to the laws of individualism and natural law. We can be grateful indeed that they failed in this objective, that the Political Union of England, the Committees of Correspondence of America, the Jacobin Clubs of France, instead of finally emancipating the popular will, flowed ultimately into a group system which premised the permanence of conflicting organizations.

For the act of "final emancipation," given the pluralism of modern life, is in fact an act of permanent dictatorship, which achieves the unity of the "general will" by imposing it through minority despotism. The success of Lenin on this count is famous, but surely it is not to be envied. Here we have one of the places where both democracy and Communism derive from a common Enlightenment view, and one of the places too where the shock of disenchantment is bound to be greater in the Communist world. It is one thing to discover pressure group lobbyists in the halls of a Congress devoted to the "will of the people." But is it not another to discover the secret police in a Moscow that has practically taken the leap from "necessity to freedom?"

III

The rationalism which emerged out of the ruins of the old European order is a complex matter, and in the sense of crisis we have had about democracy, no factor has been more significant than our disillusionment with it. The horror of lobbies and party machines has been somewhat dissipated over the course of time; we have learned to live with them, even if uneasily. But the horror of crowd psychology, of the mass media, of the irrational depths in the electorate, is keener today than ever. And yet the principle we have seen at work in the first case is also at work in the second. There has always been a large dash of collective emotion in democracy, and the notion that democracy is about to disappear because we have at last discovered it is more irrational than anything in the emotion itself.

But why should the attack on the old order have yielded so vivid an image of mass rationality? I have already hinted at a phase of the answer to this question: "reason" was the link which made possible a common judgment among individuals emancipated from the old group establishments. It was a kind of social cement. But more than this, it made possible the right judgment, according to God and nature, which meant that there was no longer a role for the old elites, for kings and aristocrats and priests. It united individuals, and it justified their government of themselves. Finally there was a third role that it played: it dissolved the whole mythology, from religion to monarchial heredity, which held the old order together. Not all critics of the order, of course, were extremists on all of these counts, and if Voltaire assailed the church with a simple rationalism, he still believed in monarchy. But as modern rationalism flowed into the democratic image it ultimately served all of these purposes. The Jacksonian "will of the people" glowed with a sense of community, democracy, and utility.

From the outset these principles were betrayed in the process of their realization. Whatever "reason" might mean, in order to develop democracy over the large extent of a nation state you needed much more than a utilitarian version of it to unite the people involved. You needed a myth fully as emotional in substance as the myth of the church or the myth of the king. And this is what, by an ironic twist which the French Revolution and its "cult of reason" shows in almost satiric fashion, democracy itself became: even "rationalism" became emotional. Here is the source of our modern anxieties in the face of the real democratic world, the fact that the historic ideas of democracy are as sensitive as religious symbols. But the problem of organizing "public opinion" over a large territory involved more than the transformation of democracy into a faith. Rousseau is our classic thinker here, and if we take his concern out of its immediate moral context, we will see again the sharpness of his empirical perception.

What troubled Rousseau was that the intimacy of the general will might not be susceptible of projection over the wide territory of the nation, so he fell back, as we know, on the small community, the Greek city. Now whatever might be said about the collective symbiosis Rousseau desired to achieve, one thing is clear: even the most primitive kind of public opinion, the kind that is needed to execute an election, to define an issue, to organize a party, was hard to come by in the Eighteenth century. The isolation of individuals and localities, physical and psychic as well, posed a real problem for the unifying function even of "natural law." In this sense Rousseau was concerned with a plain problem of communication, and it was a very important one indeed.

It was solved by a series of technical developments which have never quite been given their due in treatments of the rise of democracy. There was the growth of cities, which brought people together on a larger scale than ever before. There was the expansion of transport, which shrank the dimension of the nation state. There was, above all, the rise of cheap journalism, of newspapers that every man could buy. When the penny press was invented in Philadelphia by Christopher Conwell in 1830, and soon spread throughout the country, a cry went up on the part of genteel critics like Tocqueville. Its standards were low, its political invective almost incredible, and there is no doubt that the temper of our journalism has risen rather than fallen since that time. But this popular press, with its analogues in England and France, was indispensable for organizing the very essentials of a public opinion. Whatever its slogans were, whether "the Bank" or "the Corn Law" or the "will of the people" or *"la république,"* they provided (for all their emotionalism) the only fixed points around which popular decisions could be made.

Was the rationalism then which assailed the older order completely perverted by democracy? Was there no "progress" as men moved from the one to the other? These are subtle questions, more subtle than those involved in measuring old corporate pluralism as against democratic pluralism. For it would indeed be hard to argue, especially in light of the anxieties they have generated in our own time, that the rituals of democracy are any less ritualistic, any less superstitious, to use a more brutal word, than those of monarchy and aristocracy. The coronation of kings, Bentham to the contrary notwithstanding, was never charged with more emotional content than the reification of the people. But after this has been said, is there not surely one major difference? The symbols of monarchy are the symbols of popular submission, while those of democracy are the symbols of popular participation. The power of myth is used in radically different ways in the two cases. Nor in arriving at decisions, can we say that the rationality of interest, the Benthamite factor, has remained unchanged as we have moved into the democratic world. Whatever the emotional hullabaloo may be by which popular participation has to be implemented, out of it have come real calculations of democratic interest. It would be absurd to say, in light of all the popular social reforms of the last century, that democracy has not produced more decisions in the popular interest than the will of Eighteenth century aristocracies. "Reason" in this sense has been at work through the very medium of popular emotion.

It is unnecessary to minimize our difficulties here. The power of a great electorate to understand the technical questions of modern policy is, as Walter Lippmann and Graham Wallas began to lament after the first World War, bound to be limited. There must be a heavy reliance on the knowledge of elites. The expansion of the mass media, if it has yielded a razor-edge closeness between public opinion and government policy, has yielded also manipulative possibilities that are serious. The newspaper of the Jacksonian era could be started on a shoe-string; the newspaper of today is a big business, as is the broadcasting station as well. To prevent monopoly from functioning here is a major aspect of democratic policy. But our modern anxieties over the "mass mind" do not derive in a major sense from the realistic aspect of these policy questions. They derive instead from the collapse of our images of "rationality." From theorists of mass "contagion" and anti-individualistic irrationalism like Gustave Le Bon and Vilfredo Pareto, to mass-manipulators like Hitler, the spectre of the "crowd" has frightened the Western democrat. This is because he has never conceded to himself that without some sort of crowd his democracy could not work.

The Communist here is in the same boat, though rather a more leaky one, as was true in the case of the "general will." The Communist shares with the democrat a remarkable notion of public rationality, derived from the same Enlightenment source, but in his case several additional things are at work. In the first place he has triumphed in the backward East, where even modern media of communication have had a hard time activating populations. It is not enough to have a myth of democracy, one must have as well people who are ready to embrace it. But more than this, the centralization of communications in the hands of the state produces a frightfully overt monopoly for the manipulation of opinion in the Communist world. And that opinion is backed up by force. Under these circumstances the image of popular "rationalism" as a determinant of public policy has vastly more to hide than it does elsewhere. If we are speaking of the anxieties yielded by disenchantment on this score, surely Western democracy has reason to congratulate itself.

IV

Political equality, the idea of a state dominated by no elite and no class, has probably been "exposed" more often than any other aspect of the democratic image. Indirectly the exposure of it is related to every other phase of the anti-democratic criticism, the idea being in the case of pluralism that "pressures" and "machines" really run the state, and in the case of mass irrationalism that "demogogues" do. But the most significant muckraking on this count in the Twentieth century has undoubtedly been done by the Marxists, who have insisted that democracy is ultimately an instrument of the capitalist minority, and that the effort to use it for fundamental social reform will lead inevitably to a fascist reaction. The high point of anxiety here was reached during the 1930s, when critics like Harold J. Laski ended practically every book they wrote on a note of deep gloom.

Certainly the image of an equal state, as it evolved in the struggle against the old aristocracies of Europe, was as pure and shining a symbol as any other in the democratic myth. It was, indeed, related to the others by a logic which argument could not break. In the theory of Locke the individuals emancipated from the old group establishments, governed by a common principle of reason, had to "contract" on an equal basis to create the state apparatus. The whole theory would have been meaningless if the parties to the contract derived inequitable results from it. Nor for our purposes does it matter whether there are one or two contracts in Locke, whether there is only a social contract and the relationship between society and government is merely fiduciary. Whatever political commitments flow from the original pact must, by virtue of everything antecedent to them, be universal in their consequence. In the democratic mind, "special privilege" is the worst of political crimes.

Now when Marx framed his attack on democracy, when he announced that the state was the "executive agency of the ruling class," there was a good deal of wisdom in his view. He was writing of France under Louis Philippe, of England after the first Reform Act of 1832, and whereas these states had expanded the suffrage to some degree, there can be no question that they were heavily under the domination of capitalist power in land and industry. Nor as suffrage was extended even further in the Nineteenth century is it easy to deny that economic might was influential beyond proportion in the determination of public policy. In America the very pattern of democratic "exposure" was set during the Progressive Era of the early Twentieth century, when the cry against the "interests," not merely as they choked off opportunity but as they influenced the action of the state, was raised throughout the land.

But the situation has changed since the early Nineteenth century in Europe or the late Nineteenth century in America: the state has become more universal, and under the impact of reform movements, even differences in private income have been flattened out remarkably. What has happened is that the democratic state, originally distorted by the impact of capitalist power, has achieved a measure of universality which Marx never anticipated. The notion that our party competition is a myth because of the ulterior grip of "capitalism" on all of the parties involved, is a notion which has been dramatically refuted by the social gains of the Twentieth century. Of course the Marxist can always fall back on the argument that the "fundamentals" of capitalism have not yet been touched by the party system, as he did so often in the 1930s, and predict a Fascist catastrophe when the proletariat makes an effort to touch them. But what is "fundamental"? If the New Deal and the British Labor Party are excluded from the "fundamental" category, there is a real question as to whether we need interest ourselves in that category at all.

The truth is, as the experience of Spain and Germany and Italy show, Fascism has appeared in precisely those countries which either lacked a capitalist tradition or were late in developing one. And as we move farther East, where the authoritarianism of the left rather than the right has emerged as a problem in our time, it is again the historic absence of a capitalist middle class which forces itself upon our attention. Thus capitalism contributed enormously to democracy by helping to create a state which could ultimately transcend capitalist interest and become a genuine vehicle of popular liberty. One is reminded here of Eduard Bernstein, of late Nineteenth century Marxian "revisionism," of all the modifications of Marxian doctrine hated so much in the Leninist tradition. For it was this trend of thought, within socialism, which insisted that democracy could universalize itself through the action of the working class. Bernstein said that democracy was originally a "partnership," a queer echo of the "contract" of Locke, but that it was not a real partnership until the mass of the people had exploited the political rights which it gave them. His socialist utopia has nowhere appeared in the West, if only because capitalism has proved itself vastly more viable than any Marxist imagined. But the record of welfare legislation is proof enough that his faith in the ultimate universality of the democratic state was a sound one.

But can we say the same thing of the Marxist state as it has actually materialized in the East? In orthodox Marxism there is, of course, no symbolism of contract, itself a hated memory of the bourgeois order. The "dictatorship of the proletariat" emerges organically out of the decay of capitalism, ultimately withering away into a world where no state is needed. A stateless world is indeed a wild promise, one which the symbolism of democracy, for all of its claims, happily does not make. The concept of a stateless time is to be found in Locke and Rousseau, but they wisely place it at the beginning of things rather than at their end. But even within the context of the Marxian proletarian dictatorship as we know it in Russia and China, the dream of popular rule is matched by the fact of party despotism. Realism here is thus very explosive indeed. For if a man gives up his faith in a coercionless future, he has nothing to face but an authoritarian present. Is it any wonder that, at least in our own time, the bitterness of the alienated Communist exceeds by far the passion of the disenchanted democrat?

V

The competition between democracy and Communism that I have sketched in this essay is, I admit, a curious one, a kind of reverse competition in the process of disillusionment. There are many levels on which that competition proceeds today, military, economic, and political, and it is not my purpose to say that this one is in any sense "ultimate." But insofar as ideas play a part in the struggle, I believe that the factor we must watch is not how glowing the utopias are but how drastic are the consequences of disenchantment—what remains when the fires are out.

Compared to pleas that we "recapture the revolutionary spirit" of the Eighteenth century, this view is bound to seem unsatisfying in certain ways. For one thing it seems to give us little to do but wait until troubles have beset the Communist world. Actually this is not true. Apart from the major task of conquering our own anxieties, of defending democracy in a realistic sense (in terms of the functioning system rather than the classical image), it does not preclude the "exposure" of Communism. The realism of opposing movements is always a factor in the precipitation of insight on the part of any system. If Marx helped to make democracy aware of the power of the bourgeoisie, certainly democracy ought not to forego the pleasure of making Khrushchev aware of the tyranny of the Communist party.

Here, however, we must guard against a certain kind of disappointment. For the intellectual competition between systems proceeds by its own historic logic, which is often independent of the charges they hurl against one another. We ought not to hope for too much from "disproving" the claims of our opponents. The power of a rising system is manifest, not in the arguments it can refute, but in the arguments it can ignore. Most of the modern "exposures" of democracy were developed by the early conservatives, from Edmund Burke to Vicomte Louis de Bonald, but their arguments rarely received a reply. Democracy ignored them, simply repeated its slogans with a wilder fury. Communism has been in the same position in the Twentieth century, and if a thousand people have joined the Communist ranks for every pamphlet which conclusively "disproves" Communism, we ought to remember, on the basis of our own experience, that this situation cannot last. It is itself, in a kind of Greek fashion, the prelude to more difficult times.

When a system has become established, when it faces enemies from within and without, gradually it begins to feel the need to reply, and the age of realism appears. The replies are matched by a deepening insecurity, and there is an odd aspect of whistling in the dark, for together with the tired affirmations there are the fantastic anxieties of self discovery. Democracy reached this point some time ago, and Communism is reaching it now.

But why should both of these systems, so antagonistic to one another in the modern world, experience the same process? I have spoken of a common Enlightenment root. The truth is, intellectually we have only experienced *one* revolution in modern times, and that is the revolution of the Enlightenment. The negative idealism that liberalism forged in the fight against feudalism, with its images of individuality, rationality, and the popular will, were adapted by Marxism to the fight against liberalism. Democracy and capitalism overthrew the old corporate order with a new set of images, but Communism has tried to overthrow them with their own.

The consequence has been all manner of semantic confusion in the polemic of our time, which did not take place in the polemic of the Eighteenth century—where after all a king could pretty well be distinguished from a common man. Now we have to argue over what is "real democracy," what is "real equality." But more significant than this is the fact that when Communism appropriated the Enlightenment it appropriated also, as if in compensation for its theft, the same mechanism of idealism and self-discovery that democracy contained.

And yet: not quite the same mechanism. The triumph of Communism in the East has meant that it has taken place in an area which had no long tradition of popular participation in government. This has meant that the distance between the Communist slogans of "democracy" and the actual world has been much greater on every count than in the case of Western democracy. It has meant that the sternest despotisms have been joined to the slogans of the Eighteenth century. Moreover Marxism made some improvements on the theory of democracy in the process of taking it over: a classless, stateless, coercionless world. And so in a situation where few political promises could be fulfilled, it has multiplied their number.

Viewed against this background, the anxieties that we have experienced over witnessing democratic institutions as they actually function in the West are peculiarly fantastic. We have made the Enlightenment work in spite of itself, and surely it is time that we cease to be frightened of the mechanisms we have devised to do so. We have implemented popular government, democratic judgment, and the equal state on a scale that is remarkable by any earthly standard. There are problems here, but no "crisis," no question of "survival." In the post-Enlightenment era into which we are inevitably moving, Western democracy, if it has the courage to face itself, need not fear facing others.

New Structures of Democracy: Britain and America

By Samuel H. Beer
Harvard University

IN MODERN BRITAIN the classical image of democracy makes an uneasy fit with the realities of the distribution of political power. As Hartz has emphasized, that image was strenuously individualist. Or to put the point in a slightly different way, the classical view stressed the dispersion of power. It was hostile to the corporate bodies of the old regime and cool to newer groupings of party, class and economic interest. In contrast the real structure of political power in Britain today embraces massive concentrations—primarily, of course, in the two great political parties, but also in a set of highly organized pressure groups. One writer has been led by similar developments in another country to coin the term "organization-democracy."[1] Conventionally, however, the word to mark such contrasts is "collectivism." And while the word may initially suggest a kind of policy—for instance, the welfare state and the planned or managed economy—it also is used to refer to features of structure and organization. In this sense, one may say that a "collectivist democracy" has tended to emerge from the concentration of power that has transformed the older "individualist democracy" of the classical image.

But the problem is not merely to assess how far collectivist reality departs from the individualist image. That is an interesting historical and theoretical task. But to recognize that modern practice has broken with the older individualist modes

An earlier draft of certain descriptive portions of this essay appeared in *The Annals of the American Academy of Political and Social Science,* 319 (September, 1958), 130-140.

of action would not alter greatly the way the British think of their politics today. In this respect, the political culture of Britain differs quite a bit from that of the United States, where the classical image still has a powerful grip on the minds of ordinary citizens, if not of political scientists. For, in contrast with Victorian conceptions, a new *image* of democratic government has grown up in Britain which allows for many aspects of the new *structures,* and legitimizes them as expressions of the essential democratic ideal. This collectivist image, which as we shall see comprises a theory of party government and of functional representation, is widely accepted and acted on. Yet it is a serious question whether even this new, this collectivist, image fully and accurately reflects the realities of political power. One is uneasily reminded of the apologetics of "managerial capitalism" that attempt to show that the virtues of the individualist economy are still exhibited by an economy transformed by oligopoly.[2]

The experience of Britain in recent times provides the material for raising and illustrating these questions. And contrasts with the United States will help bring out some of the significant points of the story. Yet many of the main turns and developments, it may be said, in spite of important differences from one country to another, apply to all the Western democracies. In all, democracy on the individualist model has been modified by powerful forces. In all, its performance is challenged by severe problems. At the core of these is an old question, now more urgent than ever: How to combine a substantial degree of popular participation with a system of power capable of governing *effectively* and *coherently?* Perhaps the British have stumbled onto as practicable a solution as one is likely to find.

I

Individualism in some ultimate sense is an essential of the Western tradition. Never, one might argue, has theory been so collectivist or practice so corporate, that the individual personality has been completely absorbed in a social body— estate, class, nation, trade union, church or the like. To some extent, the individual remains always a center of influence and a repository of value. We can grant this argument, however, and still recognize distinctions. From time to time the role of the individual has been differently conceived in theory. And practice has paralleled these differing theories and the images in which they have entered the political culture of a people. In this sense, democratic and liberal theory greatly expanded the role of the individual in comparison with what it had been in the corporate and hierarchic thought of medieval and post-medieval times. Likewise, modern collectivist views have again limited and qualified an underlying individualism.

In the aristocratic England of the Eighteenth century, for instance, the relation of the House of Commons and the electorate both in theory and practice was still strongly marked by what we may call functional representation.[3] Society was composed of various "estates," "ranks," "orders" and—to use the term most commonly employed—"interests." Along with the ancient local communities, these broad functional groupings, rather than individuals, were the basic units of representation. The House of Commons was thought of as representing the landed, the commercial, the professional, the colonial and other great interests of nation and empire, and variety of franchise was defended because it enabled this variety of interests to be represented.

But if individual Members of Parliament were expected to promote such interests, this did not mean that any set of subjects were free to organize and to press their views on Parliament. Quite the contrary. Voluntary associations for political agitation—in contrast with the "fixed" and "corporate" interest groups of the society—were very close to unconstitutional. Parliamentarism—the notion that the House of Commons was a place for deliberating and reasoning on the great affairs of state—was hostile to "authoritative instructions," "mandates," and organized pressure politics on broad issues. Thus the operative ideals of the time tended to restrict the freedom of action of the individual, at once tying him closely to the established social groupings with their recognized interests, and limiting his ability to create new associations in pursuit of new demands.

Opponents of the old order were not all democrats in the strict sense of the word, but the growing demand for popular government—with or without restriction of the franchise—voiced an individualism that broke sharply with the old notions of functional representation.[4] In Britain this was true of both Liberal and Radical schools of thought and similar views can be found in the United States. The Liberals—Macaulay in Britain and Madison in the United States would be typical—remained committed to parliamentarism. For them the member of the legislature is not a delegate, but a representative, charged with deliberating on the common good. If we ask *what* is represented, however, the Liberal answer is not corporate bodies, interests, or classes, but individuals. In harmony with the individualism of their economic outlook, they thought of representation as based on the rational, independent man. In both countries the fear of interest groups was marked, especially in America where Madison in *The Federalist* gave it classic expression in his analysis of the dangers of faction.

Still closer to the heart of the classical image of democracy is the current of Radical thought. Breaking with Liberal parliamentarism, the Radical would make government the instrument of "the will of the people," a unified and authoritative force in which he found the only sovereign of the polity and for which the majority spoke. Toward any lesser grouping, toward those influences that divide the community and create partial goals, he was supremely hostile: there should be only individual "atoms," in Hartz's terms, and the state. Lesser groupings were the "special interests" or, in Bentham's phrase, the "sinister interests" against which "the people" and their champions fought. This image of "the people" against the "special interests" is the central symbol of the Radical tradition not only in the United States, but also in Britain and on the continent. Yet in spite of his stress on unity, the Radical is as rugged an individualist in politics as the Liberal. "The people" achieve their unity by a series of rational, individual acts of mind. The unit of political action is not class, estate, rank or interest, but still the rational, independent man.

II

The history of ideas cannot be chopped up into neat and mutually exclusive periods. The conceptions of authority embraced by the political culture of modern Britain inherit a great deal from the Liberal and Radical, as well as a more distant, past. Yet in this century we can discern the growing force of a contrasting cluster of sentiments and ideas which may be called the collectivist image of democracy.[5] Its major theme is party government; its minor theme, functional representation. While it has been more commonly expressed by spokesmen and members of the Labour Party, it is also widely held by Conservatives. And in newspaper comment, political debate and the results of public opinion surveys, the principal assumptions can be readily traced. This image is not confined to the closets of political philosophers, but functions as an operative ideal of daily political life.

Like the Radical, the collectivist rejects the parliamentarism of the Liberal. While Parliament has an important role in ventilating grievances and focusing attention on the large issues, it is not the place for deliberating and deciding policy. But the collectivist is not a direct democrat. Between the electorate and the Government he interposes the party, vesting it with far more authority than does the Radical. This the collectivist can do because, rejecting the older political individualism, he stresses the role of social groups: primarily classes, but also the subgroups which underlie the great vocational associations of the modern economy.

To base party upon class and vocation is very different from basing it upon the "natural consensus of free wills" which the Radical conceived to be the foundation of his organizations. Once you accept this approach, for instance, you face no problem of looking about for other like-minded individuals: your political associates are unmistakably defined as all those who share your class status. And as it becomes easy to identify your party, so also it becomes correspondingly hard to break with it. For this becomes not the simple task of dissociating yourself from certain other free men who, in your opinion, have mistaken the common good; it is rather to break with your class, an objective social fact visibly embodied in certain vocations.

Conceivably one could hold a class theory of party and yet because of the multiplicity of classes accept a multiplicity of parties. Socialists avert this blow at party government by their premise that there are only two classes, the working and the owning, and that, therefore, there is only one issue before the electorate, socialism or capitalism. But it is not only socialist theorists who think on these lines. As public opinion studies have shown, Britons in general think of the two major parties as representing respectively "the working class" and "the middle class" and display remarkable agreement in assigning the members of the main class-identified vocations to one or the other of the parties.[6]

From these premises a full-fledged theory of party government can be derived. That government should be conducted by a party to which individual MPs are bound by powerful ties of discipline is fully legitimized. Party program now can make an emphatic claim to what we may call coherence, since it is derived from a comprehensive social philosophy which relates meaningfully *all* proposed policies. Democracy is interpreted to mean, primarily, periodic contests between two such parties. While an "imperative mandate" from the local constituency is ruled out, another kind of mandate, so to speak, a collective mandate, takes its place and gives to the victorious party the right to carry out its program. Deliberation—the weighing of issues—occurs, not in Parliament, but among the electorate during an election and within the parties themselves.

Two party competition; unity among partisans in the legislature and executive; a program deriving from a distinctive social philosophy; party allegiance based primarily on economic class; a party structure allowing for participation by members in the framing of program and choice of leaders: these are the main ingredients that are condensed—and so, of course, often blurred and distorted—in the collectivist image of party government in Britain. An underlying individualism is, no doubt, retained. The individual voter still has a choice between two parties and, if he is a party member, may take part in democratic procedures within the party. In so doing he is expected to act rationally, perceiving his class interest, understanding the philosophy of the national interest that it implies, and making his choice of party and program accordingly. Yet at the same time a massive concentration of power is legitimized.

Along with this image of party government has arisen a new version of functional representation. Political theorists and advocates have not given organized groups nearly as much attention as parties, so it is not as easy to articulate the main elements. Yet when one follows the action of organized groups and their relations with one another and government, one can discern an image of group representation that is as new and as widely accepted as that of party government. One element is the recognition that it is not only legitimate, but necessary, that the great economic interests—such as workers, employers, farmers, the professions—be organized. In the history of the trade unions one may most easily trace this change in law and in the climate of opinion, but the acceptance of organization in other fields marks no less a break with individualist ideals. The proper scope of such bodies is conceived to include certain non-political functions —for instance, the collective bargaining of trade unions and employers on a national plane. But by far the most interesting development is the legitimizing of direct and continuous contact of these organizations with the executive branch of government. Again the long struggle by the trade unions for "recognition" by government departments—long after they had won recognition by employers—illustrates the point. But other groups—for instance, the teachers—have had the same fight. Today it is normal procedure for such organized vocational groups to have ready access to administrative decision making. Regularly by law representatives of such groups are associated with advisory bodies to ministers exercising delegated powers. And beyond this is a vast system of advisory committees, formal and informal, bringing representatives of trade unions, trade associations, farmers organizations and similar bodies into continuous touch with administration. That the Government has made policy without first consulting the organized interests involved, is a rare and serious charge. More than that, what is sometimes required is not merely consultation, but "negotiation."

The modes of organization and action legitimized by this image differ greatly from those of the Liberal-Radical tradition. The individualist idea worked to free political man from the restraints of the fixed, corporate groupings of the old order. The Radical view, stressing as it did that the moving force of government should come directly from the people, greatly encouraged the formation of voluntary associations for political purposes. From the early part of the Nineteenth century organizations of this sort proliferated—the Anti-Corn Law League is a good example. Thinking in terms of American experience, they were, very broadly, of the type illustrated by the Anti-Saloon League. Most had only a single purpose—or set of closely related purposes—which they urged primarily upon the legislature. And once this purpose had been achieved the association might well disband. With their individualist perspective, the members conceived themselves to be united by the specific acts of individual minds; hence, each new effort required, so to speak, a new "compact." In contrast, the typical pressure group of recent times, such as the trade union or trade association, rests on vocation, performs non-political functions and pursues a complex of related goals leading it into continuous political action. The individual, caught up in an association indissolubly connected with his livelihood, is likely to have little real freedom of choice. As with political parties, concentration of power is made legitimate.

III

That party is a mighty force in British politics is not news. The portrait of party government has been featured in accounts of British government for many years. And although the subject has only recently been given much attention, we already know that pressure groups also play an impressive role.[7] If the popular images of British democracy have also developed along the lines suggested here, it would seem that thought has merely kept step with action. Yet these new collectivist images themselves suggest that there may be facets of the actual structure of power not yet brought to light. How does functional representation fit in with party government? If in modern Britain, to echo Herman Finer's phrase, party is "king," does that make the great economic pressure group merely a courtier, offering advice and asking favors, but accepting, without influencing, the decisions handed down from above? And in general, is it possible to have such concentrations of political power and still retain the essentials of democracy?

To examine the actual structure of power in British democracy we need some sort of hypothesis to give us a suggestive start. Certain chapters of recent economic thought can, I believe, give us this help. The economy is not, of course, precisely analogous to the polity. In its way, however, as Lindblom shows in considerable detail, it is a system of social decision-making, and broad changes in its structure may suggest directions in which the political analyst should look. This is particularly true when he is interested in the consequences of concentration, since this subject has been of major concern to economists.

Liberals and Radicals brought their individualism to the study and reform of the economy as well as the polity. To both they applied their doctrine of the dispersion of power. In the Smithian model of the economy, for instance, the wealth of the nation and the satisfaction of consumers' wants will be maximized, if the market is free. And "free" means above all that no unit is to exercise "market power." In an atomized, individualized economy, all exchange will be voluntary, since no unit can coerce any other. The ruling forces will be impersonal: every buyer and seller must adapt himself to price changes and cannot control them. Power being banished; and rational, voluntary exchange enthroned, the maximum in "social efficiency" results. That is to say, the particular things the community wants will be obtained in the particular amounts they are wanted. Full use will be made of the labor supply. All resources will be so allocated between various forms of production as to maximize the satisfaction of the consumer.

Very similar to this Liberal-Radical model of the self-regulating economy is their model of the self-governing polity. Remove Burke's "established aristocracy" and all other agents of power that have historically guided the political process. Reduce society to its individual, rational atoms. Then, power removed, reason will reign. A free, competitive marketplace of ideas, automatic and self-regulating like the marketplace of the laisser-faire economy, will test the truth of opinions. Upon opinions so tested, popular government will base public policy. No one governs anyone else—no one *can* govern anyone else: the system is self-governing.

As an operative ideal and a current of folklore, this model had several variants, some of which we have touched on. Some trusted the plain people more, some less; some gave an important role to free deliberation in the legislature, some made the legislature merely the echo of "the voice of the people"; some stressed the maximizing of special interests, some the realization of a unified public will. All, however, advocated the dispersion of power. The boss-busting drive in politics paralleled the trust-busting drive in economics.

No real-life economy ever quite lived up to the criteria of the self-regulating model. Certainly, the study of the British and American economies of the past generation or two has revealed structural changes that depart radically from it. The central fact is concentration: the tendency toward the concentration of economic power among a few buyers or sellers in a particular industry or complex of industries.[8] Flowing primarily from concentration are three major consequences. The first, which concerns the internal structure of large units, is referred to by such terms as bureaucracy and managerialism. Secondly, the relations of these units tend to be marked by "bargaining," or perhaps it is better to say, "collective bargaining." Finally, while bargaining tends to be confined to the relations of large units engaged in production and distribution—which includes not only business firms, but also trade unions—those units dealing with the mass of unorganized, ultimate consumers have learned to shape, to manipulate, even to create, the very "wants" that presumably they have come into existence to satisfy. Mass advertising is, of course, the principal instrument of this sort of manipulation.

Concentration in the polity has had strikingly similar consequences: in the internal structure of large units, in their relations with one another, and in the role of the mass of voters. The collectivist tendencies of economic structure find suggestive, if not precise, parallels in the collectivist tendencies of political structures. In these terms, a comparison can be made between the actual structure of power and the collectivist image of democracy. In these terms also comparison can be made between the structure of political power in Britain and in the United States. It appears that as tendencies toward collectivism in economic structure have gone farther in Britain than in the United States, so also have those toward political collectivism.

But there is a further reason why this analysis and comparison should be of value to the person concerned with the structure and effectiveness of American democracy. In this country many people, practicing politicians as well as political scientists, are much troubled by what they regard as an excessive dispersion of power. In particular the advocates of party government argue that reforms bringing our practice rather closer to the British will make our system at once more democratic and more effective. Perhaps they have taken the British image of party government too much at face value. The reality may be less wholly attractive. Yet the problem that concerns these critics of the American system remains: the need for a coherent and effective policy. To analyze the British system is to present a more sober and realistic view of the possibilities that are open, of the choices that can be made. Such choices rarely do include an ideal alternative.

IV

That power is more highly concentrated in British than in American parties is such a commonplace it hardly seems worth elaborating. One index of concentration in political organizations is density—that is, the percentage of eligibles brought in as members. Judged simply by nominal party "memberships" in the two countries, American parties may well exceed British. If, however, we give party membership some meaning by adding a qualification, such as regular payment of dues, then it is obvious that British parties have mobilized the electorate far more highly than have ours. Another measurement that would be practicable is amalgamation, taking this to mean the number of independent organizations into which the persons organized are grouped. Such an index would distinguish the multi-party from the two-party countries, but would not show much contrast between Britain and America, except for the fact that the former has a more substantial third party.

Given the fact that the British is essentially a two party system and that it has organized at least as large a part of the electorate as the American, what makes the British system more concentrated is the far greater capacity of its parties for unified action. In the loose and sprawling American party, power is dispersed among many poorly articulated units—personal followings, state and local organizations, and the like. The result is that only occasionally and for limited purposes, such as nominating a presidential candidate, does the national party act as a unit. In the British party too, there are semi-autonomous centers of power that a perfect merger would obliterate: the typical local association, for instance, will not stand having its choice of candidate dictated by central headquarters. Yet the contrasts with American practice are weighty and familiar. We think of the fact that all candidates for Parliament must be approved by a central party agency; that they will all accept and run on the same platform; that in general when a party takes a stand on an issue in Parliament or in the country, it does so through an agreed spokesman and with a single voice. No doubt the most striking expression of this power of united action is the degree of party voting in the House of Commons. Judged even by A. Lawrence Lowell's strict criteria, party voting, which has been on the increase for a century, today is so close to one hundred per cent that it is hardly worth measuring.[9]

To see that British parties act with unity does not, however, tell us how this unity in action is achieved. Each party has an elaborate and effective system of articulation, in particular representative bodies extending from bottom to top and a bureaucratic staff running from top to bottom. It is clear that central party leaders enjoy far greater power within their respective parties than in the United States. In both British parties, as R. T. McKenzie has shown, the leaders of the parliamentary party, and especially the Leader, are dominant.[10] That is a loose description and needs must be as the relationship is shifting and complex. Leaders cannot "ignore with impunity the moods and aspirations of their followers; they must carry their followers (and above all, their followers in the parliamentary party) with them. And to do so, they have to take into account at every stage the clearly defined currents of opinion within their party."[11] The Leader of a party must continually practice what Sir Ivor Jennings calls "the art of management,"[12] appeasing a dissident faction, finding a formula of agreement, keeping up morale. Indeed he is a "manager"—a modern day manager committed to certain organizational purposes, of course, but by his situation compelled continually to devote himself to holding together and to keeping in running order this large and complex organization. His role embraces many of "the functions of the executive" in the large and established business corporation, as Chester Barnard has described them.[13]

Consider how a modern leader rises. In Victorian times one common method was by championing some reform or cause and building up himself a following in the country as well as Parliament that compelled the other leaders to take him in. Randolph Churchill brilliantly followed this tactic, even though in the end he overreached himself. So also did Joseph Chamberlain, whose grip on Birmingham was so great that when he broke with the Liberals, he carried the city with him into alliance with the enemy—surely an inconceivable event today. This Victorian type was not unlike the entrepreneur building up his business in the unorganized and growing economy. But today, although political entrepreneurs have not utterly vanished—Aneurin Bevan comes to mind—the aspiring politician is much more likely to rise through what one Labour MP has called "the career mechanism." You do not disrupt the party and ruin your future by going off on a personal crusade. You accept and advocate the party program, much as your opposite number in a big business may sell the products that his firm has developed through its routine research procedures. This program is not the invention of any single person, but the output of "the party mill," in the phrase of a prominent party leader.

Correspondingly, motivation itself tends to change. W. L. Guttsman in a study of the aristocracy and the middle class in the British political elite in later Victorian and Edwardian times has detected an interesting contrast.[14] Broadly it is between the aristocratic types who were mainly motivated by an interest in the exercise of power, and middle class types more concerned with forwarding a cause or reform. The managerial leader is a third type: to use a popular phrase, he is "the organization man" in politics. The goal of power, but especially the goal of long-run power for the party, shapes his motives. We may compare the "professionalism" of business management which "precisely because it is in business to make money years on end, cannot concentrate exclusively on making money here and now."[15]

In this brief sketch, two points may be stressed. First, the mass of dues-paying members, not to mention the greater body of regular party voters, take no active part in this interplay of influence within the party. Dues-paying members in Britain run into the millions; active party members number only thousands. In the local association there is "an oligarchy of the faithful" who regularly attend meetings, hold office, choose candidates and otherwise perform and direct the work of the party. These may have influence, sometimes through the representative bodies of the party, but more likely through the parliamentary party. It is in the latter arena and especially among its leaders that the principal decisions are made. Secondly, these leaders are professionals—little as this may be to the liking of the older traditions of British politics. Almost without exception they are full-time politicians and have a kind of professional code, the code of the mass party organization.

V

Turning from parties to pressure groups, we find that in Britain as in the United States the center of the stage is occupied by organizations based on the great economic interests of modern society. These are especially the big three of business, labor, and agriculture, although we cannot neglect the professions—doctors, teachers, civil servants, and others. Public policy has become collectivist: the programs of the welfare state and the managed economy affect these interests directly and continuously and the rise of organizations representing them has proceeded in no small part from this expansion of policy.

Such collectivist pressure groups, as we have seen, are bureaucratic in structure and vocational in their social bases, in contrast with the typical pressure groups of Victorian days. Another and parallel distinction is suggestive. If sociology can take seriously the distinction between "self-oriented" and "collectivity-oriented" action, political science may also find it useful. Essentially the distinction is between action aiming at an advantage primarily to the actor and action aiming at an advantage primarily to others. The extremes are rarely found in reality: pure egoism is as scarce as pure altruism. Quite apart from propaganda, self-oriented groups in British and American politics normally view their interests as linked up with the interests of others. Conversely, the group pressing for some advantage to others rarely sees this action as incompatible with its own long-run interests. The difference is one of emphasis, but it has consequences for structure and behavior. The collectivity-oriented group, for instance, is open to all like-minded persons, while the self-oriented has, so to speak, a fixed clientele. By and large the self-oriented group can more readily extract money and work from its members on a continuing and regularized basis. It is also less likely to splinter and more capable of continuous, unified action.

This distinction runs very close to the classification of British pressure groups into "interest" groups and "promotional" groups made by Professor S. E. Finer. Among the former he would classify such organizations as the Federation of British Industries, the Trades Union Congress, the National Farmers Union, the British Medical Association, the National Union of Teachers, the British Legion, the National and Local Government Officers' Association. As "promo-

tional" groups he would include the Howard League for
Penal Reform, the National Council for Civil Liberties, the
Peace Pledge Union, the Campaign for the Limitation of
Secret Powers. As compared with the self-oriented groups,
he writes, the latter "do not represent 'interests' in the same
sense at all. They represent a cause, not a social or economic
'stake' in society."[16]

Even in this brief enumeration we cannot fail to observe
how few really significant organizations fall into the promotional rather than the self-oriented category.[17] A hundred
years or so ago, the reverse would have been true. While the
great pressure groups of the Liberal-Radical tradition often
had an identifiable social base, they were not at all the
frank advocates of vocational interest that modern collectivist
types are. And there was about their agitation a reformist tone
that is today mainly associated with the promotional pressure
group or, indeed, the political party. One line of development in the history of British pressure groups has been from
the promotional to the self-oriented, vocational type—a line
that corresponds to the general emergence of collectivist from
individualist modes of political action.

A similar development has taken place in the United States.
But with pressure groups as with parties, concentration has
gone farther in Britain than in this country. There, almost
without exception, the big vocational pressure groups have
higher indices of density and amalgamation. For instance,
the National Farmers Union is the only significant organization of farmers and includes ninety per cent of its potential membership. Such other farm pressure groups as exist
—a dissident group has tried to form in Wales—have little
or no access to the administration. In the United States, of
course, only a fraction—no more than thirty per cent—of
all farmers are organized and these are divided among three
main groups and various minor ones, which, however, often
are granted access. While absolute numbers are much smaller
in Britain, we must remember that British agriculture is highly
diversified as to crops, size of farms, and location. Yet
through the NFU British farmers speak with one voice to
a degree rarely achieved by farmers in the United States.

No doubt this is true because to no small extent the organization is run from the top. In Bedford Square is a large and able bureaucracy and at its head stands one of the ablest managers in modern Britain, Lord Netherthorpe (formerly Sir James Turner)—sometimes known as the "Sacred Bull of British Agriculture."

In the field of trade unions, just a little less than half the total working force has been organized in Britain, while in the United States the figure is around a quarter. To one peak organization, the Trades Union Congress, nearly all unions are affiliated and it has been the undisputed spokesman for organized labor for generations. Its permanent secretary, even when Walter Citrine held the post, has never occupied the position of, say, a Samuel Gompers. The heads of the Big Three,[18] however, have had as prominent a political role as our Reuther, Meany and Lewis have played. The British labor leaders of this generation are more likely to have worked their way up the bureaucratic ladder by long and able management than to have emerged from heroic struggles for the right to organize or for better contracts. Contrary to popular impression and in strong contrast with American experience, the strike has practically ceased to be an instrument of labor-management relations in Britain since as far back as 1932.[19] If by bureaucracy, however, we mean full-time paid staff, then British unions generally are far less well endowed than American. The reluctance of the rank and file to pay dues sufficient to employ such a staff—and to pay substantial salaries to any permanent official—seriously handicaps British unions.[20]

In the field of business, in Britain as in the United States the basic unit of political action is the trade association, although it should be observed that there the differentiation of function between the employers association and the association for other purposes has been far more consistently carried out. Comparison is made a little easier if we consider only national manufacturing trade associations.[21] Of these there are 1,300 in Britain as compared with some 950 in the United States. Density is high among the British groups: a sample survey showed that 90% of larger firms and 76%

of smaller firms belong to one or more such associations. The peak association is the Federation of British Industries, which represents through its affiliated trade associations and directly through member firms some 85% of all manufacturing concerns employing ten or more workers.[22] In the United States, on the other hand, the National Association of Manufacturers has never represented more than 6% of all manufacturing concerns.[23] If the same base as that used for the FBI were taken, there is reason to think that the NAM figure would be more like 20% to 25%. The contrast would still be striking.

The British Employers Confederation embraces associations whose firms employ about 70% of all industrial employees in private enterprise. Measured by this standard, the NAM compares fairly well: its members employ about half of all industrial employees in the United States. This contrast between the relatively small number of firms included in the NAM and the high proportion of employees represented by them suggests—what has often enough been said—that the NAM represents big business rather than business as a whole. If so, it appears that small business is better organized at the national level, or at least more fully represented, in Britain than in the United States. The point could be generalized: small farmers also are quite highly mobilized, while this does not seem to be the case in the United States. Probably the same can be said of unskilled workers in the two countries.

VI

So much for the briefest sort of sketch of concentration in the British polity and its consequences on internal structures. Let us now turn to the modes of interaction of these massive units.

Given such concentration, the typical relationship between units will surely differ radically from what it would be if there were little or no political organization, or if the reality represented something like the classical image as Hartz has sketched it. With some help from the concept of "bargaining" developed by economists, we can isolate the features that result from such differences in structure. This term is used to describe relations among units where there is competition

among the few—the title of the principal book on the subject.[24] It refers to direct negotiation between a few large
organized units—as between a large buyer and a large seller,
or between two firms similarly placed—and also to cases
where there is not direct negotiation but tacit bargaining.
In a free market, impersonal forces rule, because no unit
controls enough of supply or demand to affect significantly
the outcome—the market price. In a bargaining situation this
is not so: each unit controls a substantial fraction of supply
or demand; hence can significantly affect the outcome. Each,
in short, has some "market power."

The self-regulating polity of the individualist tradition
presents a suggestive analogy with the free market. For the
sake of illustration one may think of the impersonal forces
arising from the fierce competition of a wide-open American
primary election with its bidding for votes by candidates and
for promises by voters. In contrast, the relations of pressure groups and political parties of the collectivist type par-
take of the nature of open or tacit bargaining. The party has
—or hopes to have—the whole power of government. The
pressure group controls something the party needs—a substantial block of votes or perhaps something more subtle,
but no less essential, such as the hearty cooperation of the
group in carrying out an economic policy. The situation is
not likely to be one of straight bilateral political monopoly.
There will be another party in the competition and also other
pressure groups. But the control, or prospective control, by
each side of a substantial fraction of what the other side
wants makes for bargaining. It has been said by those who
have sat in on the Annual Price Review in Britain between
the National Farmers Union and the Ministry of Agriculture
that the proceedings and the way in which a settlement is
reached resemble nothing so much as collective bargaining
in the field of labor relations. Again, when we examine the
relations of ministers and trade union leaders in the periods
of "wage restraint," the process of demands, concessions, and
give and take on both sides has much in common with the
familiar bargaining process between representatives of union
and employers.

The method and spirit of bargaining affect all the main

phases of policy-making in the collectivist polity. That point, however, at which it is most readily identified is where the pressure group is brought into contact directly with the executive branch of government. Such consultation with interests is a feature of all modern Western democratic governments. Some years ago Avery Leiserson, writing of representative advisory committees, traced their origin to "the delegation of discretionary rule-making powers under legislative standards to administrative agencies executing various types of social legislation," and observed that in the United States the committee device had been conceived in Wisconsin shortly before the first World War.[25] Leiserson's statement, broadened somewhat, is a generalization valid for not only American, but also for Western European government: increasing government intervention for such purposes as social reform, economic stability and national defense has led to the grant of rule-making power to administrative agencies and to increasing participation of interested groups in decision-making at that level.

Different stages in this development, however, can be distinguished, depending upon how far the scope of policy has been expanded and the polity has become collectivist. The extent to which power has been mobilized and unified on each side—on the side of the party in power and on the side of the pressure group with which it deals—will determine whether bargaining predominates in the relationship. In the United States we find administrative consultation on a vast scale both in Washington and in the state capitals. In Britain, a more collectivist polity, the situation is better described as "quasi-corporatism."

It is against the background of this pattern of power that we must examine the emphasis that British pressure groups give to the various points in the process of decision-making. The formal structure of authority—British parliamentary government as compared with the American separation of powers—will play its role. But we must recall that a hundred years ago Britain also had parliamentary government, yet pressure groups then gave far more attention to the legislature than they do now.

VII

In each polity we may distinguish four main phases of policy-making: at elections, in the legislature, within the party, and at the administrative level. British pressure groups exert their major influence at the administrative level, taking this to include both ministerial and official contacts. Perhaps their second most important point of influence is within the party. In comparison American pressure groups, by and large, give greater attention to the electorate and the legislature.

There are, of course, many variations within these two broad patterns. In either polity the more legal authority delegated to an agency, the more likely it is that the relevant group will devote attention to it. A very important difference may result from the character of the power base of a group. For example, the group that is strong in the technical advice needed by an agency, but weak in votes, will probably find the administrative approach the most effective.

There is also a kind of power—and this is particularly important in Britain—that is created by the expansion of policy itself. "The greater the degree of detailed and technical control the government seeks to exert over industrial and commercial interests," E. P. Herring wrote, "the greater must be their degree of consent and active participation in the very process of regulation, if regulation is to be effective or successful."[26] This generalization, I should think, holds for most Western democracies and surely for Britain. There, certain types of control exercised in recent years—price control, materials allocation, tariffs, import control, and the encouragement of exports and productivity are only some of the more striking examples—simply could not have been enforced without the substantial cooperation of the groups concerned. The group's technical advice is often well-nigh indispensable. But cooperation—something more than grudging consent to "the law"—is a further necessity. Our farm programs with their referenda and farmer-elected committees recognize this necessity. But in Britain the far wider scope of regulation and planning—even after the various "bonfires of controls"—gives this power factor far greater weight.

Neither the British nor the American system of consultation between government and pressure groups has been fully described. Some rough impressions, modestly intended, may be in order. In both countries a central device is the representative advisory committee. British examples range from high level bodies—such as the Economic Planning Board, the National Joint Advisory Council of the Ministry of Labour, the National Production Advisory Council on Industry—on which the relevant peak organizations, the Federation of British Industries, the British Employers Confederation, and the Trades Union Congress are represented, to the multitude of advisory committees of the main economic departments to which trade associations often send representatives. The latter are connected with the system of "sponsoring" departments which grew up during and after the war and which means today that every industry and every branch of it, no matter how small, has a sponsoring department or section of one, somewhere in the government machine. In 1949 Clement Attlee, reporting on advisory committees including outside persons, said that at the center they numbered about seven hundred—in addition to which was an untold number advising central government departments in various localities. Apart from such committees, although often around them, a regular system of informal consultation has grown up. Private and public bureaucrats continually call one another on the telephone or meet for luncheon and discuss a problem on a first name basis. Often several departments and several groups are concerned. Once they have bargained out a solution, we may note, it is far from easy for the minister, who has the formal power of approval, to reject the proposal and start the whole process over again.

On the American side, it is clear that from the time of NRA in 1933, the use of the advisory committee, from being relatively rare, has immensely increased.[27] The number of advisory committees associated with government departments at the center—in addition to many more at the local or regional level—runs into the hundreds. One major set, established by statute, is in the Department of Agriculture—for instance, the Commodity Stabilization Committees. Of the remainder, the vast majority are non-statutory and associated principally with the defense effort—procurement, development, standards, stockpiling and so on—consisting of industry advisory committees in the Departments of Commerce and Interior, General Services Administration, or Defense Department.

In comparison with the British industry advisory committees, most of the American committees depend far more specifically on defense. Their numbers swelled during World War II and again during the Korean war, but greatly diminished in peacetime. Likewise, in composition the American committees make much less use of trade associations. This is a result at least in part of the Defense Production Act of 1950 which requires that non-members as well as members of trade associations be included. And in general, there is, as compared with Britain, a pronounced hostility to permitting officials of trade associations to serve on the committees. The peak associations—the NAM and the United States Chamber of Commerce—play virtually no role in this structure, again in contrast with their British counterparts. Similarly, trade unions are given far less formal recognition than they enjoy in British committees. The TUC alone, for instance, is represented on some sixty committees touching all aspects of social and economic problems. In Washington there is nothing faintly like this degree of recognition and broad and continuous formal consultation.

Of the broad character of the power relationship we can speak with confidence: the American executive is far from having the dominance over political decisions that the British enjoys. Quite apart from the lesser degree of delegated powers in this country, the political independence of Congress and the exercise of administrative oversight by Congressional committees mean that the group interested in influencing policy must give great attention to the legislature. Some years ago, Donald C. Blaisdell found that pressure groups, while concerned with administration, focused their attention principally upon Congress.[28] Broadly, this is still the case. Although in the last generation or so, they have given increasing attention to the executive branch, it still remains that their efforts to influence the legislature constitute "the most obvious actions of pressure groups."[29]

VIII

Americans do not like to think of their parties as representing social classes, but we can underestimate the degree to which big labor and big business find their friends on different sides of the party fence. In 1956, for example, the contributions of organized labor to presidential and congressional candidates favored Democrats as overwhelmingly as business contributions did Republicans.[30] Similarly, while the number of trade union officials sitting as delegates at Democratic National Conventions has run into the hundreds, the number at the Republican conventions has been negligible. Yet in spite of this alignment of labor and business with the two American parties, an important distinction from British structure remains. This does not consist only in the open and formal affiliation of British trade unions with the Labour Party. The important point is, that in the United States these groups exert themselves to influence individual candidates rather than the party organizations as such. Our national party platforms have some importance, but in general American parties are so poorly unified that they cannot provide an effective channel for influencing the use of government authority. In Britain, on the other hand, the party organization ranks second—though still perhaps only a poor second—to the administration as an object of interest group pressure.

Where the power is, there the pressure will be applied. Where we see pressure being applied, therefore, we shall probably find the seat of power. Pressure groups do not openly descend on a British party conference as they do on the platform hearings of an American convention. Their representatives will be present, however, and spokesmen for various special interests—farmers, trade unionists, veterans, teachers, old age pensioners, advertising men with a concern for commercial television—will take up a good deal of time at a party conference. But the important point of influence is the parliamentary party—its regular, full meetings and its specialized committees.

We are familiar with the way leaders of the Labour Party while in power or in opposition will frequently consult with the trade unions on pending decisions. There is also an active alignment, if not formal affiliation, of organized business with the Conservatives. During the passage of the bill nationalizing transport in 1946–7, for instance, the Conservative opposition offered several hundred amendments. Where had they come from? In practice, the party's Parliamentary Secretariat—a body of party employees, not MP's—acted as intermediary between the transport committee of the Parliamentary Conservative party and the various pressure groups, especially the General Council of British Shipping, the Dock and Harbors Association, and a joint committee of the Federation of British Industries, National Union of Manufacturers, and the Association of British Chambers of Commerce.[31]

Inseparable from these channels of influence is one of the —to an American—most curious phenomena of British politics. He is the "interested MP"—that is, the member who is connected with an outside interest group by direct personal involvement, such as vocation or ownership of property, or by membership or office-holding in an outside organization speaking for an interest group. Today and for generations the House of Commons through the personal involvement of its members has represented a far wider range of interests than has the American Congress. The American legislature is notoriously inhabited by lawyers, although we should note that this is less true of the state legislatures, especially in the advanced industrial states such as Michigan and Pennsylvania.

In Britain such personal involvement was a principal way in which interest groups of the Nineteenth century made themselves heard in government. Of more importance in today's collectivist polity is the member connected with an outside organization. The MP's sponsored and subsidized by the trade unions are the best-known examples. But there are also a host of others: a joint honorary secretary of the Association of British Chambers of Commerce, the chairman of the Howard League for Penal Reform, former officers of the British Iron and Steel Federation, a vice president of the Association of Municipal Councils, a director of the Society of Motor Manufacturers and Traders, the President of the British Legion, the secretary of the National Tyre Distributors Association, the treasurer of the Institute of Bankers, a past president of the Residential Hotels Association—there seems to be hardly a member who fails to note some such connection in his biography in the *Times' House of Commons*. Perhaps some Congressmen also have similar connections. Amid their wide membership in churches, fraternal organizations and "patriotic" groups as recorded in the *Congressional Directory*, however, they fail to mention them. If these connections do exist, this failure to record in itself is not insignificant.

Perhaps, as S. E. Finer has suggested, the absence of such interested members from the Congress is one reason why American pressure groups must make up the deficiency by hiring lobbyists in such large numbers. For the interested MP is an active lobbyist within the legislature. His principal role is played within the parliamentary party, but his activity in the House itself is more observable. He may speak openly as the representative of a group, as the president of the British Legion often did in forwarding the Legion's campaign to increase disability pensions.[32] He is more likely to be effective in the amendment stage of a finance or other bill when, briefed by his association, he suggests changes, which perhaps at the same time are being urged on the minister and civil servants by the officers or staff of the pressure group. A combination of approaches is normal: pressure on officials and ministers; when that approach seems to need further support, agitation within one or both parliamentary parties, especially their specialized committees; open advocacy by an interested MP at the amendment stage. Ministers do yield; if not in "principle," at least in "details" that may make all the difference to the particular interests concerned.

IX

Long ago E. P. Herring observed how American pressure groups direct great attention to influencing public opinion, in order not only to win support for some immediate objective, but also to build up generally favorable attitudes. This he found to be a trait of the "new" lobby, and it is not irrelevant that this technique arose along with modern mass advertising methods and media. The tendency has continued. "The most significant recent development in pressure group activity," according to Hugh A. Turner, is "the continual increase in the efforts of interest groups to win support for their organizations and programs by using the mass media of communication to influence public attitudes."[33] And he goes on to describe how many business organizations, labor unions, farm groups and professional associations hire public relations experts to advise their top planning bodies and to direct propaganda campaigns.

What about British practice? At one time, in the hey-day of the Liberal-Radical pressure groups, the campaign to influence public opinion was a common thing and as a result many of the major reforms of the early and middle part of the Nineteenth century were initiated and pressed through successfully. Beginning later in the century, however, this propagandist function seems more and more to have passed to the political parties. In recent decades, the parties have virtually monopolized communication with the voters as such —that is, with the general public as distinguished from communication by a pressure group with its clientele. Pressure groups, of course, keep in touch with their members through regularly published periodicals, meetings of representative bodies, and the like. But this is, so to speak, propaganda internal to the group. Overwhelmingly, organizational efforts to influence the electorate at large have been confined to the parties.

This differentiation of function has had important consequences. For without in any degree being cynical one may acknowledge the large part played by British parties in creating the present homogeneity of the British electorate—the national market for their brand-name goods. The British party battle is continuous and highly organized and so is the stream of propaganda directed at the voter. Quite apart from party publications and canvassing by party workers, the press forwards this effort by reporting the words and deeds of partisans in Parliament and outside. Thus the party voter is strengthened, if not created, and the tight party majority in the legislature prepared. Even more important, the framework of public thinking about policy, the voters' sense of the alternatives, is in large degree fixed from above. "The effect of party management today," Nigel Nicolson writes, is "to use all modern means of mass-communication to create a mass mind which does not require to think and therefore ceases to discriminate." Radio, television, popular newspapers and general education, he says, instead of facilitating the process of discovering, instructing and expressing the public's point-of-view, have "merely served to stamp it out from two huge rounded moulds." Thus the attitudes that divide the parties "are themselves the product of constant party warfare."[34] The danger is that popular sovereignty in the polity may be modified by the same technique of manipulation that modifies consumer sovereignty in the economy.

To talk of public opinion being manipulated or manufactured irresistibly conjures up the notion of dark, designing "power elites" cleverly controlling the masses, perhaps by tapping deep springs of irrationalism in the "crowd." That would be a caricature of reality. Yet we cannot fail to sense in Britain the extent to which the classical function of party has been reversed. That function is, of course, to transmit the wishes of the voter to the centers of authority. But the modern party also performs another function: it makes what the state is doing acceptable to the voter. Of course, the parties differ and on that basis criticize one another. But on the main elements of collectivist policy—the welfare state and the managed economy—they are substantially agreed. And day in and day out, they are praising—for example, while taking credit for—these policies, arguing for their necessity, excusing them plausibly when they cannot praise, finding their results on the whole good and full of health. This surely is no small force conditioning the citizen to accept the new social and economic order.

Yet we cannot take this pattern of influence as fixed. The public campaign has sometimes been used by the big pressure groups of British politics and its use may well be on the increase. The great expansion of the public relations business in Britain in very recent years at any rate provides the tools.

Examples of recent campaigns are the anti-nationalization campaign launched by the Road Haulage Association in 1946–7; Tate and Lyle's famous "Mr. Cube" campaign against the nationalization of sugar refining in 1949–50; the vast campaigns of institutional advertising mounted in very recent years by the steel and chemical industries concerned with the threat of nationalization; and in general the growing use of *Aims of Industry,* a public relations agency founded to defend and advocate free enterprise.

Here surely is a facet of British politics that deserves watching. So far the practice has not much affected the pattern of power. The anti-nationalization campaigns, for instance, hardly do more than extend and intensify positions being pressed by the Conservatives. But neither party's goals are merely a reflection of the economic interests aligned with it. Both principle and tactics often guide party policy in quite a different direction. If the propaganda of pressure groups were to bring out these differences, pressing them on voters by continuous campaigns, conceivably the power of the parties could be shaken. Such a development might bring the British pattern closer to the American. For we can hardly say that our politics is any freer of propaganda and high-powered public relations. As in other aspects of the American power pattern, the difference is that the centers from which this weighty influence emanates are far more dispersed and uncoordinated.

X

These tendencies to managerialism, bargaining, and manipulation qualify further the already qualified individualism of the collectivist image of democracy. We can imagine a political system in which they are the wholly dominant forces. Obviously in Britain today the picture is not so simple, nor so dark.

The collectivist image recognized that the individual does not enter an atomized and unorganized political arena in which each lone combatant has something like an equal chance of influencing others. Two avenues of influence, however, were left to him: first, the participation within the party and the vocational pressure group; second, a choice between parties. In reality intra-organization participation is severely restricted by managerialism and bureaucracy. Within the parties, for instance, only a small fraction of the electorate exercises direct influence on party action. Yet this is not an insignificant influence. The necessity for leaders to "manage" means among other things that they must compromise with currents of opinion in their parliamentary followings and indeed in the party outside parliament.

The opportunity to choose between two competing parties has been given more stress. Democracy, as some writers have observed, lies not within parties, but between them. The collectivist party system, it is said, enhances democracy by giving the voter a "meaningful choice." Party program means that he has a choice between lines of policy that are intelligible and different. Party unity means that he can hold responsible the candidates of the majority party for what government has done. But the internal structure of parties is not irrelevant to their external function in the political system. Even where—and indeed because—there is intense competition, managerialism may greatly water down the meaningful choice between programs. Preoccupied with the pursuit of power for their organization, party managers may, openly or tacitly, so bargain out proposals with interest groups as to make their programs very much alike on many points. And in fact in recent years the party struggle in Britain has consisted far less of pitched battles of opposing social philosophies than of small raids to capture votes from particular groups.

But even if party policies do not embrace something so grand as opposing social philosophies, they do, even in this time of relative political quiescence, reflect significantly different tendencies. There is a Conservative and a Labour point of view, continually defined and reshaped by decisions taken while in power and in opposition. Among the leaders of a British party there is an acceptance of a broad scheme of priorities which is intelligible to the average voter and distinguishable from the views of their rivals. Party manifestoes, usually the products of hasty drafting and acute electoral compulsions, are not the best sources of light on these priorities. But we cannot imagine, for instance, that the Labour

Party, if in power in similar circumstances, would have let unemployment rise as the Tories did during 1957–59 and, on the other hand, have attached such overwhelming importance to price stability.

Given these differing party tendencies, the individual voter is provided with a firm tool for choosing which tendency is to control policy by the stern unity of the parliamentary parties. Latter-day Radicals may lament the MP's loss of independence, and clamor for more "free votes." Quite apart from being hopeless nostalgia, these protests fail to show how a loose, individualist party could cope with the massive concentrations of economic power confronting government and bring them to accept the discipline of a public policy adequate to the urgent problems of the day. But this leads to the final question to be raised by this essay.

XI

Two questions may be asked of modern democracy: how democratic is it? and, can it do the job? This essay has been mainly concerned with the first. Yet the second cannot be entirely neglected.

Democratic government, like any form of government, is an instrument for solving problems. It is a means by which a community defends itself, fosters its economic prosperity and in other ways promotes what it conceives to be the general welfare. In any particular instance, therefore, we will judge it not only by how far it is democratic, but also by its success as a problem-solving device.

But by what criteria shall we judge that a system governs well or ill? What constitute the goals of the general welfare and how best to achieve them are precisely the questions around which the disagreements of democratic politics revolve. Whether an economic policy is wise or unwise will be judged differently by the socialist and the Tory, by the liberal Democrat and the conservative Republican. Must our critique of political institutions depend on such partisan perspectives? This would imply that one structure of democratic power would suit a certain line of partisan policy better than another —Tory purposes better than socialist, or conservative Republican than liberal Democrat—while another structure would show a different bias. And surely such a bias can sometimes be detected. David B. Truman, for instance, has observed how the dispersion of power in American democracy favors the "defensive" interests. E. E. Schattschneider has argued that for several generations from 1865 to 1932, the tendency of our system to inaction was precisely the policy most desired by the dominant, conservative forces of American politics. The structure of power suited their aims of policy.[35] As has often been contended, the American system does make positive government difficult. Perhaps indeed what we have is a conservative polity, and those who criticize are just liberals masquerading as political scientists.

Yet surely we also feel that there are capacities that partisans of both Right and Left—the democratic Right and the democratic Left—wish to see displayed by the instrument of government; that there are some basic criteria that both sides would agree on. This is one thing we mean by saying that the democratic state is "neutral," or that, as Hartz puts it, "universality" has been achieved. The instrument will carry out equally well the will of either party and does not display a bias that is more favorable to one line of policy than another. If we are to make a scholarly and non-partisan critique of our own institutions, we need to articulate these criteria. We would then have a basis for evaluating one distribution of power as compared with another.

In these concluding pages, I can do no more than sketch these standards and the reasons for thinking that the American system satisfies them less well than the British. If one word were to be chosen that suggests them, it would be *efficiency*. The notion is complex, but it has been given a certain degree of precision in its application to the performance of the economy. In simplest terms, it means getting the most for the least: the best possible use of resources toward achieving your goals. It is such a notion as this that we have in mind when we ask that our system of government be not only responsible —that is, democratic— but also effective. It will clarify the idea if we examine two of its components: the criteria of *coherence* and of *innovation*. Surely, both the Right and Left in either Britain or the United States would agree that the instrument of government should have (1) the capacity to produce policies that are coherent within each field and over the whole area of governing; and (2) the capacity to identify new problems and make such innovations as may be called for.

One can think of these criteria abstractly, for they are qualities of success in any process of problem-solving: without being grandiose, one can say they are canons of the logic of problem-solving. An individual, for instance, in dealing with his problems of daily concern will try to adopt means that produce the ends he seeks; to make the various steps he is taking, so far as possible, not only consistent with one another, but also mutually supporting; to allocate his resources so as to give priority to the more critical means and more important ends. So far as he succeeds, his solutions have coherence: there is a deliberate definition of ends and a rational adjustment of means to ends.[36]

How would this abstraction be applied to the process of government? For the sake of illustration we may take an example from the field of public administration. The purpose of the control of expenditure, it can be said, is to achieve "balance" in the programs financed by that expenditure. Strictly, this would be satisfied only when expenditures were so distributed that the last dollar spent on each program produced the same amount of public good. In practice, balance means that expenditure should not be extravagant in one sphere and parsimonious in another. And, of course, before the standards can be applied to decisions, it must be informed by a scheme of priorities in terms of which services can be judged more or less necessary and expenditures extravagant or parsimonious. Left and Right will differ on the scheme of priorities; both will agree that "balance," along with the administrative structures that promote it, is desirable.

To say that a system of problem-solving must have the capacity to innovate, does not mean that it *ought* to innovate. That would be importing a partisan or ideological preference into a standard that we should like to keep relatively objective. But anyone will agree that success involves being able to perceive new circumstances when they arise, determine if they are relevant to your goals, and devise those new and creative solutions that will promote your purposes. A system, like an individual, needs this power of innovation for survival. Again, of course, we need to say that in the field of government the particular goals in the light of which problems are identified may differ according to partisan perspective. And the need for creative adaptation may arise not only from the pressure of changed circumstance, but also from the rise of new interests and ideals within such a partisan perspective. In any case, the power to adapt, to be flexible, to move swiftly and creatively, is one that no government faced with the problems at home and abroad of the present age can wish to be without.

In the light of these criteria of coherence and the potential for innovation, how do different structures of power—such as those we have touched on in this paper—affect the output of policy? Here I would echo one of the most familiar criticisms of the American system. Its dispersion of power creates strong tendencies to incoherence and immobilism. In contrast, the concentration of power in the British system—while not ideally democratic nor by any means perfectly efficient—increases the opportunity for coherent and creative solutions.

The tendency to inaction in the American system flows in part from the formal structure of authority. For instance, to get through a piece of legislation in Washington—or a state capital—you must win a favorable decision at some half dozen or so critical points: one or more committees in both Houses; the votes of the whole body in both legislative branches; the chief executive, and perhaps more important, his principal advisers in the relevant agencies. Other things being equal, the chances of the group interested in preventing action are far greater than those of the group favoring it. The contrast with the British system is obvious. But the contrast, as this inquiry has been concerned to show, is not one of formal structure alone. On the plane of parties and pressure groups, power in the United States is also fragmented and dispersed. This means that, as Walter Bagehot remarked of unorganized legislative bodies, "the greatest difficulty [is] in getting, not only a right decision, but *any* decision at all."

The nub of the trouble is the absence of firm party majorities. Lacking them the tendency to delay, indecision, and immobilism arises. When decisions are made, they are likely to be the product not of a party majority, but of what A. N. Holcombe calls a "casual majority"—one composed of followers of both parties whose views happen to coincide on the particular question before the legislature at the moment. But a series of such "casual majorities" is almost sure to produce policy that is incoherent. Nowadays all major aspects of policy, foreign and domestic, affect one another. What is done in one sphere will promote or retard what is being attempted in another: consider the interrelations of domestic economic policy and foreign economic policy, farm policy and inflation policy, policy toward our allies abroad and policy toward industry at home. Government decisions consist not only of the particular votes on each policy or aspect of policy, but also of the resulting pattern of such decisions. When "casual majorities" pronounce successively upon our national affairs, there may be no pattern, no coherence. So, for instance, what one decision on foreign aid attempts to build, another decision on tariffs may tear down. The long-run program set up one year may be eliminated the next year—or what is almost as bad, threatened with elimination—before it has had a chance to prove what it can or cannot do toward achieving its goals. In a time that requires the utmost in efficient, long-run performance from our instrument of government, it fails to provide the base for "a sustained flow of political power."[37]

For a generation or more this failure has become increasingly apparent. In 1936 E. P. Herring wrote—

"A democracy inclines toward chaos rather than toward order. The representative principle, if logically followed, leads to infinite diversity rather than ultimate unity. Since the 'voice of the people' is a pleasant fancy and not a present fact, the impulse for positive political action must be deliberately imposed at some strategic point, if democracy is to succeed as a form of government."[38]

Democracy and Economic Structure

By Charles E. Lindblom
Yale University

THE DAZZLING PRODUCTIVITY of the American economy since World War II has blinded some of its erstwhile critics. Even in 1958, when job hunters outnumbered jobs and, most dramatically, a slump in automobile sales proved that all that glitters is not sold, the mood of economic euphoria was only mildly dampened. We have been congratulating ourselves, however, largely on the economy's output; how the output is achieved excites no special admiration and, on the contrary, stirs a few anxieties. Large national product, a bounteous flow of richly varied consumer goods, and a high rate of new investment—these we applaud. The possibilities that we are the dupes of cunning admen, that big business is overly influential in Washington, that trade union power is neither harnessed nor sufficiently self-disciplined, and that continued prosperity rests on military spending all trouble us; and we do not know whether these and other possibilities like them represent minor skin infections or deep malignancies in democratic politics.

It is therefore appropriate that we reflect not only on the efficiency of the American economy but also on the lines of control that run through it and connect it with government. Who runs the economy and how? What are the relations between power holders in the economy and power holders in government? In asking such questions as these, we shall be examining economic structure not in the economist's language of calculation but in the political scientist's language of power.

Some characterizations of certain power relations in politico-economic life like James Burnham's thesis of the managerial elite or C. Wright Mills' thesis of business-military power are developed without any reference at all to certain other obviously important opposing lines of control, such as consumer control over sellers.[1] If read as comprehensive analyses of power in the economy, they are constantly misleading. If read as partial analyses, they do not identify the larger context of power relations into which the analyzed relations are supposed to fit and thus cannot be integrated into a larger organized knowledge of power in the economy. In neither case, therefore, do they make a substantial contribution to the cumulation of knowledge. Hence the frequency with which such theses come and go without leaving a lasting imprint.

It is all the more important to be comprehensive in examining power in politico-economic life because the central institution of economic life, the market or price system, typically drops out of analyses as though it were irrelevant to the study of power. Even if economists did not prove the point by using terms like "purchasing power," "bargaining power" and "monopoly power," it ought to be obvious that the market or price system is a power system; it is a system for controlling behavior; within it are to be found leaders or elites as well as a rank-and-file; and it embraces a variety of interpersonal controls, including coercion.

I. Power in the Price System

To use Hartz's term, there is one common "image" of the price system that leads those who hold it to assert a fundamental incompatibility between economy and democracy. In broadest terms, efficiency and democracy are viewed as in conflict. More precisely it is argued that the price system, or market economic organizations, is inherently undemocratic in its concentration of power in the hands of businessmen —managers and entrepreneurs—who are neither themselves popularly elected nor appointed by popularly elected officials and whose businesses are "their own business" rather than a public trust.

But professional economists have produced at least two other images of the price system that have come to be widely held in society. The first is an image of what a price system might be if its potential were more fully realized. It is the price system seen as a system of delegated authority in which leaders hold particular powers subject to a kind of vote, a system about which such questions can be asked as: Do the leaders have to satisfy the voters as a condition of staying "in office"? Do leaders compete for followings? Can an incumbent be removed by an unfavorable vote?

So conceived, the price system is a political system something like government in which certain powers lie in the hands of a small active decision-making elite called businessmen. It is for them to decide directly both how much is to be produced of each good and what combination of labor, equipment, and other factors of production is to be used. In large-scale business, they coordinate a cooperative productive process embracing many thousands of participants.

If this elite manipulates the economy, it is seen as doing so only in a responsible and responsive way. For when a consumer makes a purchase, his expenditure constitutes a vote for continuing the line of production on which his money is spent. A businessman can only sell what people will buy, which means that their refusal to buy will effectively veto his policies while their willingness to buy gives him a mandate to continue. The entrepreneurial elite cannot long go on producing anything that does not win the dollar votes of the market place.

Markets are of course tied together in long chains so that some businessmen look for votes from (sell to) other businessmen who look for votes among still others, and so forth, as, for example, in a series of markets connecting the extraction of iron ore with smelting, steel making, auto manufacturing, and auto retailing. In this respect this image of market democracy is a system of soviets.

A significant characteristic of voting in the market, so envisaged, is that voters usually canot vote for a particular member of the governing elite whose personality or style of policy-making they like; they must instead vote for or against his individual policies. One can not vote for the president of

General Motors but can vote for a two-toned red and cream Chevrolet convertible hardtop with white walls, heater, radio and power steering.

Market voting is similar to voting in the democratic state in that the initiative in policy-making lies in the hands of the governing elite rather than the voter. What leaders initiate is eventually controlled by reaction to their policies at the polls and, in the interim, by each leader's anticipation of electoral response.*

In the democratic state, political leaders control each other by exchanging favors, threatening and promising, organizing alliances, opposing or supporting each other's policies. These moves are understandable only against the background of the competition for votes; on the other hand, they are worth mentioning as methods by which leaders are controlled by other leaders rather than by voters. Similarly, in the present image of the market businessmen control each other in a variety of ways that might escape our attention if we thought only of direct consumer and supplier control over market leadership. They buy from and sell to each other; beyond that they frustrate or assist each other's plans in various ways. Similarity between state and market in this respect is illustrated in the ubiquity of bargaining in both.

Given the two conflicting images—price system as authori-

---

*Still other differences and similarities between market voting and balloting will quickly spring to mind. Of the differences, one most significant is that in the market the electorate is double-headed. Just as each member of the entrepreneurial elite is competing for the consumers' dollars, he is also competing for their productive services. Hence the same individuals who control the businessman through offering or denying him their consumer votes control him again by offering or denying him their labor, their capital, or other services and goods he needs as factors of production. When we speak, as is commonplace, of consumer sovereignty in the market economy, we sometimes forget about this equivalent supplier sovereignty; but the businessman is constrained in some decisions just as surely by the preferences of his suppliers as he is in other decisions by the preferences of those who buy from him. Because almost every member of the businessman's electorate is both a demander and a supplier, each "voter" has two heads.

tarian and price system as comparable to political democracy
with respect to its internal power structure—how does the
price system actually function? Although its actual functioning does not correspond closely to either of the two conflicting images, it corresponds well to still another image that
economists have produced. This is an extremely complex and
sophisticated image that takes account of a variety of specific
discrepancies between what is ideal or potential and what has
been so far achieved. Because the image is complex we cannot describe it with a few words but will instead suggest how
it takes account of various troublesome features of real world
economic organization not recognized in the economist's first
image.

A. BUSINESS RESPONSE TO CONSUMER PREFERENCES

In this second image, it is acknowledged that business management is not invariably responsive to expressed consumer
preferences. Just as in government votes can be incorrectly
counted, so also in the market the vote can be misrepresented
through price manipulation. And just as in government a
well-entrenched machine may show indifference to the electorate so also in the market a well-entrenched cartel may
similarly show indifference to its consumer electorate. Where
in government an incumbent may be secure against an effective challenge from another party or candidate, so also in the
market the competitor may also be unchallenged. In short,
the image recognizes monopoly.

But the image, being sophisticated and close to the facts,
also perceives limits on monopoly. No firm can charge any
price it wants or even approximate such power; consequently
no firm's monopoly power is ever absolute. One of the most
important foundation principles of economics is that *all* goods
compete with one another for the consumer's dollars; hence,
as the price of any one good rises, at least some buyers turn
from it to others, and the seller is consequently constrained.
All goods compete, whether peanuts and wrist watches or
carpets and bobby pins, simply because in allocating his in-

come a consumer will move away from items whose prices are too high even if he cannot find a close substitute.

Monopoly is also everywhere constrained by forces more powerful than the very general competition of all goods with one another. In advanced societies technology has made close substitutes of steel, copper, aluminum, glass, rubber and plastic. While they cannot in each of their uses be substituted one for the other, in many uses at least one can be substituted for another. Hence the attempt to manipulate price or restrict output for any one of them is restricted by the certainty that at least some part of the market will be lost. Moreover, in a wealthy economy in which consumer income goes into durable goods like autos and refrigerators, monopolistic exploitation of the consumer is greatly restrained by the consumer's ability to use what he has for another few years rather than buy a new model. For some consumer durables this control is supplemented by highly organized second-hand markets to which consumers can always turn to escape monopoly over new products.

B. Manipulation of the Consumer

The image also takes account of the fact that businessmen manipulate the preferences of the consumer electorate. Everywhere at hand is evidence—the renaissance of cigar smoking, for example—of the success with which the economic governing elite manipulates the preferences of the consumer electorate rather than simply respond to existing preferences. On the other hand, in this image it is recognized that what the elite does not attempt to do, as well as their conspicuous failure—the Continental and Edsel fiascos, for example—satisfies us that their manipulative powers are not unlimited. Still, if it were true, as is sometimes naively believed, that the more the manipulation, the less the democracy, it would be clear that democracy in the market was in poor health. But, just as we ask for some disclosure of record and program from each candidate for governmental office, we want information from businessmen about their products, and we want it *because* we expect it to influence our preferences. Without much doubt, therefore, some kinds of manipulation of preferences by governing elites are not inconsistent with democratic ideas.

C. INCOME INEQUALITY

In the image under discussion, it is recognized that incomes are unequally distributed, and those who hold this image concede that at least some forms of income inequality are not consistent with a view of the price system as democratic. But does the one man-one vote rule in political democracy require by analogy an equal distribution of money votes?

Political democracy does not require equality of the vote in all decision-making situations. On the ground of expediency and of their special concerns, we give to the inhabitants of certain areas—a town, for example—voting powers denied to all non-residents, even though non-residents have a stake in the decisions reached, as is the case with local street maintenance and traffic control. For some decisions on agricultural policy, we poll limited groups of farmers. For determination of bargaining units in industry, we poll limited groups of wage earners.

Sometimes, however, it is said that democracy requires, not equal power and not equal votes, but equal votes at the point at which the decisions are made on who will have specialized powers and unequal voting power. In other words, the argument runs, the democratic ideal does not require that you and I be equally powered generally but only that you and I have an equal vote in the determination (directly, or through election of officials) of when and where you or I shall have greater power than the other. But even this "last say" equality of the vote can be challenged as a requisite of democracy. We neither practice it in the United States nor agree that we should, as is illustrated in practices and attitudes on constitutional amendment. Moreover, it can be powerfully argued that democracy is better characterized as government resting on consent than as government resting on "last say" voting equality; and consent is won by conceding disproportionate powers to groups who must be wooed.

Thus, in the United States, behind a superficial appearance of one man-one vote, lies a variety of arrangements, including the bicameral legislature and the electoral college, that in effect give some citizens a voting power far in excess of that of others.

To be sure, not all the inequalities in voting power in our government are the product of the search for consent; and, even for those that are, some observers would argue that they represent imperfections in democracy which can be avoided only in the ideal democracy in which consent can be won without sacrificing "last say" equality. I simply record that political democracy is not *agreed* to require equality of the vote and that we practice extreme inequality in "last say" voting power in the United States.

Analogy will therefore not prove equality of the dollar vote to be a requirement of market democracy. Is there, then, some other ground on which equality of the dollar vote is required for market democracy? If we consider the equalitarian tradition that has developed in Western civilization, we see that, powerful as it is, it is nevertheless severely limited by the acknowledged need, as in the case of political equality in particular, for functional specialization, as well as by the desirability of certain other kinds of inequality. On close examination, the tradition is not so well characterized as a belief in equality as in opposition to certain specific kinds of inequality. Especially when the tradition is articulated in a politically effective movement does it appear not as a generalized push to more equality but as an attack on specific troublemaking inequalities: legal privilege at one stage, racial discrimination at another, for example.

The inequalities we have held to be intolerable are those that make one man an instrument of another; foster personal traits of arrogance, insensitivity, harshness and defensiveness, on one hand, and obsequiousness, apathy and hostility, on the other; create arbitrary marks of superiority and inferiority and proliferate other invidious distinctions; leave the individual without minimum requirements of food, shelter, health and education; obstruct functional specialization; or create disruptive social cleavages. The list covers a great deal; nevertheless, it does specify. Some differences in "who gets what" create these problems, but some do not.

D. Undemocratic Employee Relations

The image also takes account of common failures in the achievement of "industrial democracy" in the market. Many people, who, never having conceived of the price system as a potentially democratic system for the consumer, will raise no questions about consumer democracy, will nevertheless question the authoritarian character of the employer-employee relation. If democracy exists in the economy, they will say, it exists because it is to be found in the employer-employee relationship; if the market is undemocratic, it is simply because the employer-employee relationship is undemocratic. In the present image of the price system, however, are some grounds for claiming that the system is not fundamentally undemocratic even in the employment relation.

1. *The price system is itself a method of achieving industrial democracy.* This falls strangely on ears accustomed to hearing of the market as the great barrier to industrial democracy. But if we think of higher wages as one of the major demands made by employees on businessmen ever since the development of the factory system in the United States, the fact is that this demand has repeatedly been made effective through the market. The explanation of rising wage rates in the history of the United States—or in any other country—does not turn on the labor union, for unionism has been shown to have had only a marginal influence on the historical course of wages. Wage increases in pre-union times are large, repeated and not demonstrably less impressive than under unionism.[2] The explanation, of course, is that, just as businessmen compete for the consumers' dollars, they also compete for labor; hence workers do in fact, all dogma to the contrary, exercise enormous control over employer decisions on wage rates even in the absence of a union.

The market, however, does not by any means give employees all they want in wages; and it is less satisfactory in its mechanisms for democratic control over working conditions, discipline, and individual rights and privileges on the job. If the beginning of wisdom is the recognition of the price system's limited but significant democratic accomplishments for the employee, the next step is the identification of inevitable limitations on democratic worker control, with which the next propositions deal.

2. *Many limitations on worker control of employer are attributable to the employer's responsiveness to democratic consumer controls over him.* Why does an employer resist high wage demands? Because beyond some point he can collect the funds for wage disbursements only by accomplishing a monopolistic control over prices charged his customers. Why does he resist demands to maintain obsolete skills, keep his men on the payroll in depression, or make expansive improvements in working conditions? Often because competitive controls in the hands of consumers press him to cut prices and costs. The problem here is not that the employer is undemocratic, but that his electorate is, as we said, double-headed; and he cannot satisfy both heads at once.

This fact calls for a reorientation of much policy discussion. Since what is at issue is not democratic control or none but conflicting demands made by an electorate working through two different channels upon the same leadership, the distribution of rights and controls between the consumer head and the employee head of the electorate cannot be decided by reference to traditional democratic criteria. It is possible, however, that study of this conflict might provide a basis for an extension of democratic criteria, to resolve problems of aggregating democratic demands upon leadership when the demands are inconsistent. To take an example, can democratic theory be refined or extended to throw light on how to resolve conflict between consumer and employee interest in the employee demand for a guaranteed annual wage? Similar problems of aggregating arise in democratic control in government.

3. *Because of conflicts of interest among groups of workers many demands made in the name of industrial democracy are invalid.* It is argued, for example, that democracy requires the union shop. If the relevant electorate is taken to be the

employees of a given plant and a majority of them wish a union shop, it can be argued that a union shop is democratic. If the relevant electorate is taken to be all wage earners who have an interest in employment in the plant and a majority of these do not want the union shop, the reverse could be argued. If it is held that the union shop issue is of such general importance that all wage earners in the economy are the relevant electorate, then whether the union shop is democratic or not depends on their wishes. Or if it is held that the union shop issue contains implications for efficiency or industrial peace such that consumers too—in fact, the whole governmental electorate—are the relevant electorate, then whether the union shop is democratic depends upon the decision reached by democratic governmental procedures.

While I am inclined to believe the union shop is generally desirable, my point here is that its merits cannot be argued by reference to the criteria of democracy, and we cannot say that an employer who resists the union shop is undemocratic. Similarly, demands for seniority and craft control of certain jobs cannot be argued on democratic criteria. Now again, as in the case of consumer-employee conflict, conflict among different groups of workers might be explored to see whether democratic criteria can be extended to resolve the issues. In the case of the union shop, for example, one might attack as a problem in theory the question of which of the various alternatives is the relevant electorate. Although some exploratory work of this kind would be worthwhile, the field may turn out to be a morass. It will probably be more profitable to analyze most worker demands upon the employer not in the language of democracy at all but as technical, administrative and organizational problems that have democratic solutions only in that their solutions are ultimately achieved within the framework of democratic government.

4. *Other than the market mechanism, the union has become the major instrument through which industrial democracy is strengthened or weakened.* This obvious proposition introduces some perplexing issues. We are all familiar with union accomplishments in protecting the employee against arbitrary, even whimsical, acts of the employer that impinge

upon what almost everyone will agree are democratic rights, if not rights that are essential to minimum dignity and self-respect. Without deprecating these achievements, I pass them by simply because they are familiar. The perplexing issues arise out of other aspects of unionism.

The first issue is what powers unions should enjoy. Given what we have been saying about conflict between consumer and employee and between different groups of wage earners, the appropriate powers for unions cannot be derived, except on some minor issues, from democratic criteria. In other words, what powers to allocate to unions is a technical administrative question, and any one of a large number of alternative decisions on union powers is quite consistent with democratic criteria. Any one of many possible decisions about union power can be shown to satisfy the "democratic" demands of some group, but always at the expense of some other. Although this too presents a challenge to democratic theorists, they may, again, not be able to come up with any better answer, even after careful exploration of possibilities of extending and refining democratic formulae, than that whatever allocation of power to unions is sanctioned by democratic governmental processes is democratic.

Another group of issues is concerned with democracy within the union. Unionism has not solved the problem of protecting the individual against abuse by the leaders of a large organization of which he is a part. In trying to solve the problem in the case of the employer, unionism has created a similar problem in the case of the union leader himself. A somewhat different problem is union membership control over union policies the immediate responsibility for which has to be delegated to leadership. Without characterizing unionism as generally deficient on these two scores, I am safe in saying that some large unions have been grossly deficient.

All this and more is familiar. Let me go on therefore to raise the question of whether the root of the evil, where it occurs, is rank-and-file apathy or non-participation, as is often believed. Apathy there is indeed; but governmental democracy survives in the face of it, and it has been argued that a large non-participating section of the electorate is desirable in governmental democracy.[3] Why then might union apathy be dangerous? One possible answer is that there is more of it; that is, the level of participation in unions is much lower than the level of voting in, say, a congressional election. If, however, we compare daily involvement in union and in governmental affairs or compare voting rates in union and governmental elections, it is not so clear that union members are less participating. Perhaps apathy in the union permits internal democracy to degenerate because there are no institutional devices, such as a two-party system, to keep the doors open for political activity within the union when the members wish it.[4] In government, a low level of participation is not a barrier to a high rate if the occasion demands it.

Such hypotheses suggest what a rich field for research lies at hand here, research not only to clarify the prerequisites for internal union democracy, which are not yet well understood, but also to contribute to a more general theory of the prerequisites of democracy. The study by Lipset, Trow and Coleman of the Typographical Union is an admirable and distinguished beginning to what ought to be a thoroughly cultivated research field.[5]

As for achieving more vigorous union democracy, a straw in the wind is a shift in union attention from conflicts on which the union is homogeneously set against employer to conflicts among groups within the union who differ in skill, rates of pay, seniority or other attributes. In the new responsibilities of unionism to achieve a democratic adjustment of internal group conflict lies a possibility that an internal political pluralism will flourish, bringing with it the rivalries that make democracy possible.

Union leaders will presumably be held responsible to their own members by a shifting combination of three major devices: democratic constitutionalism within the union, government restriction on union officials, and members' rights to withdraw. The third of these is, of course, presently declining. Some interesting though quite unfinished attempts have been made by union leaders themselves to argue the superiority of constitutional democracy over democracy through right of withdrawal;[6] the choice presents extremely interesting theoretical issues that ought to be explored by professional theorists. Similarly, government restrictions on trade union leaders designed to make internal democracy effective raise, in a context in which results can be observed, some traditional questions on the possibility of imposing democracy from above. Then too, insofar as government chooses to sanction the union shop and other restrictions on rights of withdrawal, the union moves from a status as voluntary organization into a yet undefined status as quasi-public agency. Here again are theoretical issues as well as possibilities for empirical study. .

5. *Finally, industrial democracy is not correctly argued to be absent simply because production is large scale and bureaucratized, relations among participants impersonal, and responsible participation in decision-making limited to a few.* Bureaucracy, impersonality, and non-participation are in large part products of technology. These phenomena are to be found in the economies of all industrialized nations and are to be taken as describing the environment in which modern democracy is called upon to operate. They are not therefore evidence of the absence of democracy in industry.

For fear of going far afield, I pass these phenomena by with but one comment. It is not clear that employees wish to be responsible participants in decision-making; their wish that some of the union representatives be so does not imply that they wish to be so themselves. Employee aspirations in this respect may differ greatly from period to period, depending upon the degree to which economic insecurity weighs upon their minds and threatens them with family financial responsibilities they fear they cannot successfully bear. On the hypothesis that employee aspirations toward responsible participation are directly related to their responsibilities and opportunities off the job, I should like to see some research on the variables determining the desire for responsible participation. Its practical fruits would be to locate sources of unrest in industrial relations, as well as to determine how responsible participation can be had when needed, as, for example, to meet demands for supervisory and managerial personnel.

E. PRICE SYSTEM AND EFFICIENCY

In the light of Beer's interest in the "efficiency" of demo-cratic policy making, it may be worth asking: Is a price system an efficient policy-making system? In the depression of the 1930's, it was not, but in recent decades it would be difficult to argue that it has not achieved a tolerably high degree of both coherence and innovation. If opinions differ on this question, they will most probably reveal subtle differences in meanings attached to Beer's term. If I mean by "efficiency" the achievement of a set of policies—that is, for the price system, a set of outputs and a pattern of income distribution—that suits my particular preferences, I rate the system's achieved efficiency rather low. If, on the other hand, I mean by "efficiency" that the system has achieved the satisfaction of the expressed preferences of its electorate in a relatively systematic manner with a reasonable minimum of inconsistency among policies, I must rate its efficiency tolerably high. Here "high" means high relative only to other complex human attempts at efficient policy-making rather than high relative to ideals toward which we might aspire.

And, it might be added for what light it throws on Beer's hopes for the achievement of efficiency in governmental affairs, such efficiency as is achieved in the direction of production and distribution in the price system is in large part, though by no means entirely, achieved without a central mind or direction that sees the interrelations of the economy as a coherent whole.

F. SOME INFERENCES ABOUT DEMOCRACY

The upshot of this discussion of power in the price system is not that the system is or is not democratic. If we think of political democracy as an attribute of a "government" and play no tricks with the word "government," then the price system is neither democratic nor undemocratic; it is simply a different kind of animal altogether. Our discussion of the image of the price system as a system of relations between leaders or officials, on one side, and a rank and file or electorate, on the other, has served only to show that, if one does wish to consider the price system in terms parallel to those in which we consider political democracy, several very important conclusions seem justified. First, it is not at all obvious that, so considered, the price system is an undemocratic element in conflict, because of its authoritarian character, with political democracy. Second, those who hold unusually large powers in the price system are invariably subject to some kind of "popular" controls, even if the effectiveness of these controls is in dispute. Third, the characteristic imperfections in popular control in a price system are analogous to the imperfections of popular control in government, and they include those that other essays in this volume have thought important to mention as contemporary problems in democratic government, such as, for example, manipulation of the electorate by leadership and incoherence in policy making. Finally, the price system, so considered, is democratic or undemocratic depending upon one's standard of appraisal in the same way that our institutions for political democracy in government are or are not democratic, depending upon one's standard of appraisal.

We are justified, therefore, in continuing to discuss economic structure and democracy without yielding to the superficial view that economic structure is itself so undemocratic as to make such a discussion fruitless.

II. Impact of Economic Structure on Democracy in Government

Having explored democracy within the economic structure, we now consider the consequences of economic structure for democracy in government, beginning with the roles of business leadership and corporation executives in political democracy.

A. BUSINESS LEADERSHIP AND THE CORPORATION

It is hard to know where to begin in discussing corporate

leadership and political democracy. We have such theses as Burnham's and Mills' to tell us that business leadership enjoys disproportionate power. But that we certainly already knew. Large-scale democracy requires and is marked by a high degree of specialization of leadership, and indeed one can even define a leader as one who has disproportionate power. We also know that there are at least some limits to the power of these leaders from the business elite. They do not suppress elections; they show dismay at the powers denied them, and they complain about the power of the union leader and professional politician.

Both Burnham and Mills neglect to analyze controls over business leadership.[7] They do not do so because they are both captives of the notion that power is fixed in amount; what the elite gains in power the non-elite loses. Believing in this lump-of-power fallacy, it is sufficient, if one wishes to prove the degeneration of democracy, to show new powers in the hands of the governing elite. We know this is too simple; it is possible at one and the same time both to increase the powers in the hands of the elite and to increase the controls held over them by the non-elite.[8]

We are not at all interested, therefore, in whether the powers of corporate leaders are disproportionate. What we want to know is to what degree their powers are inconsistent with democracy in government. Not only do elitist theories fail us; what is worse, we have no adequate criteria by which to decide even if we could agree on the facts. For as we saw in discussing the business elite in the market, and as Pennock has shown in detail elsewhere in this volume, we lack an adequate theory of the appropriate functions of leadership in democracy. Failing such a theory, we do not know, for example, whether there was any valid ground for complaint on Eisenhower's "six millionaires and a plumber," as his early Cabinet was described.

The corporate executive in non-elective office. Let us see just what is required both in mastery of fact and theory beyond what has already been specified in the discussion of business manipulation of consumers. Consider, for example, the phenomenon of businessmen in non-elective office. Political scientists should find many challenges in the frequency with which high administrative positions in government are filled by corporate executives. Arnold A. Rogow has recently argued for the British economy that the tasks of economic regulation make it necessary for government to lean very heavily on the skills and experience of businessmen in high office.[9] This thesis generalized is itself worth investigations to determine in just what circumstances it holds. In a period of rapid nationalization and extension of other regulation it would seem more plausible than today in the United States, and it hardly explains the frequency of appointment of businessmen to Cabinet and other high posts in American government in one administration after another. Why so few appointments from executive positions in the union movement? Why not substantially more appointments both from slightly lower administrative positions in government and from the ranks of the politicos?

One can smile knowingly and say the answer is clear. But I doubt it. A relative consistency in frequency of recruitment from corporate circles running from a Hoover through a Truman administration belies some of the obvious explanations, and not wholly absent variations in frequency belie others. I believe that research could help us disentangle and set out systematically the influence on recruitment of such factors as the use of appointments to repay campaign contributions, beliefs that business skills are required, public identification of union but not business leaders as partisan, unwillingness of some politicos to accept executive positions, and traditional distrust of abilities of civil servants.

It will be important to uncover the motives that lead prospective appointees from various groups to accept or decline. We may be able to document the hypothesis that far from grasping power, the corporate elite accepts government administrative duties somewhat reluctantly, being urged more insistently to do so because recruitment from the worlds of labor and of politics is difficult.

For the case of Britain, Rogow and others have also argued that businessmen are incapable of a sufficient change in role to avoid a very subtle sabotage of programs that they as businessmen disapprove of. Here certainly research is now merely scratching at the surface. How do businessmen see their role when they move into public office? What is their own testimony, and what are the objective indications of any change in attitudes, loyalties, and feelings of responsibility? In what terms do they conceive of the public interest before and after they move to government? How do they compare themselves in these respects with other public officials recruited from other circles?[10] For recruits from union circles or other interest groups, we should ask the same questions.

Roughly, the kind of hypothesis that research might verify is that in moving from business into high government administrative posts businessmen do drop some of their former organizational loyalties and pick up new ones, do act as "neutral" public servants in policies on which they can be unambiguously and explicitly directed, but nevertheless carry into and employ in their new positions previously held values and attitudes. Such findings as these could, of course, be made more precise.

If research produced such findings, it would then be important to try to achieve a systematic statement about the degree to which the decisions of such officials are locked into position by the political forces that surround them and, conversely, the degree to which the officials hold important discretionary authority in the exercise of which their business-oriented values and attitudes are operative. Many scholars have a feel for the facts on this point; but formalized, systematic statement is required if this information is to be fitted into a larger comprehension of leadership in democracy.

To construct such a systematic statement, one might begin from widespread agreement that there is no objective "public interest." What values, whose interests, should then govern the decisions of administrative officials? In the literature of political science are conflicting answers that specify what the model must cope with.[11] The administrator should be governed by the wishes of the majority. But majority sentiment is simply not known on countless problems, and citizens are dependent upon advice from leadership where they are asked to express themselves. The administrator should do what is best. But this requires him to weigh and evaluate conflicting preferences in the light of his own personal set of values. The administrator should be frankly partisan. But this is defensible only to the degree that other partisans can influence him. The administrator should follow the directive of his superior. But the superior cannot avoid leaving his subordinate some important discretion. The administrator should be guided by a party position worked out and enforced through strongly disciplined parties. But, again, the best worked out party line still leaves room for discretion.

The problem is not simply that there are alternative views or images of democratic leadership, for we can build many corresponding models. It is also that no one of the alternative views on the administrator is well enough worked out in the literature. What is required is a set of propositions, model, or—as Hartz might be willing to say—a professional analytical image that would lay out explicitly the relations most significant for democracy and place the administrator in them. Such a model or set of propositions must specify the preferences, interests or values; the discretionary range of choice; the constraints on choice; and the characteristic agenda for each of the following: voter, interest group, party leader, legislator, legislative group, various interdependent administrators, and president. The propositions must interrelate all these in an interaction process in which preferences and policy-making act on each other.

Now, again, many political scientists have a feel for this set of interrelationships; some carry the required model in their heads in the form of beliefs that they have never wholly articulated; and others have gone quite far in the direction of writing it down.[12] So while constructing the explicit formal model is a big order, it is neither impossible nor uncongenial to the skills of political scientists. My emphasis on getting such models or images out in the open, making them formal, is that we have no adequate criteria, except very fragmentary ones, that permit us to record reasons for believing that businessmen (or any other recruits from an interest group) in high administrative office do or do not constitute a problem for democracy.

The corporate influence on the social preconditions of de-

mocracy. Turning now to a quite different influence on democracy, we can distinguish several ways in which corporate policy seems consequential for democracy.

1. The manipulation of employees. In its discovery that an employee is an extremely complex machine whose output is sensitive to the most subtle changes in handling, the corporation may have learned more than it ought to be allowed to know. The discovery pays off in increased output and more contented employees, but potentially it also strikes at what may be a precondition of democracy. For probably much of what we believe about democracy and its advantages rests on the assumption that the human personality is moulded by a wide variety of competing influences, including family, school, neighborhood, friends, and acquaintances, books and newspapers. We would be hard pressed to make sense of democracy if any one homogeneous group of political leaders moulded our preferences to suit their needs, then turned around and conspicuously satisfied the demands they had taught us to make upon them. We would find it only slightly less troublesome to reconcile with traditional notions of democracy our indoctrination by a homogeneous group of leaders who held power to manipulate our personalities and preferences grossly disproportionate relative to other competing influences. Yet this disproportion is what the human relations movement may introduce. This is one aspect of the large problem of manipulation of the masses by a few.

Many critics of democracy have long been disturbed by the disproportionate influence of wealth and business enterprise on the mass media and other instruments of manipulation of the electorate. But the human relations movement makes the disproportion greater. Heretofore competitive appeals to our minds and emotions have been addressed to us as citizens not as employees. If business had disproportionate influence, it was when it sought either to influence our political activity or to encourage non-participation where we were thought dangerous to business interests. Whatever the degree of disproportion in influence, it was therefore to some significant degree limited by the competing appeals of unions, churches, farm organizations and various other special interest groups, as well as by internal conflict within business itself. The new appeal, to the employee not the citizens, is not equally constrained.

Three aspects of the new appeal to employees are significant. First, to a high degree employers agree among themselves, hence they reinforce each other's indoctrinations. Second, not even the union may be much disposed to counter the appeals because they do not ask for action that the union opposes. Third, since the businessman is motivated by the desire to make the individual an efficient instrument of production rather than a citizen ally, it may be that he will try to influence the individual more assiduously than ever before —more assiduously, because man as a tool is a better investment than man as a citizen. These, then, are three grounds for fearing that corporate indoctrination of large elements of the population may go much further than has ever before been possible, seriously violating the traditional democratic "competition of ideas."

But if these three aspects of the new appeals imply that they can be made more effectively than ever before, perhaps the appeals themselves are innocuous. This is what we do not know; for the time being the human relations movement does indeed appear to be more helpful in uncovering problems than in giving direction to a questionable program of indoctrination. It is the potential more than the present accomplishment that raises questions. For in a persistent desire to find how to make employees content and productive, the danger is that the appeals themselves will in effect encourage uncritical loyalty, obedience and passivity and will discourage independence, resourcefulness and responsibility.[13] In these respects it is feared that they undermine some of the social preconditions of democracy.

These misgivings about the human relations movement suggest several lines of research, not all of which are we yet equipped to undertake successfully. What kind of competition of ideas and of indoctrination does democracy require? What personality characteristics are required for democracy? Is the ideal employee a good citizen? What impact does the human relations movement have upon personalities of employees? Like other questions raised, these questions call for greater formalization of present knowledge as well as extension of empirical observation.

The possibility that indoctrination of the individual as an instrument of production will be more profitable than his indoctrination as a citizen raises a distantly related question so important for democracy that I mention it here somewhat out of context. As the businessman may find it more profitable to invest in instrument of production than in citizen, so in the larger political arena totalitarian rulers find it profitable to invest in their citizens as instruments of production where democratic rulers seem to think it unprofitable to invest in them as citizens. Hence, as we have discovered, the Soviets more rigorously pursue education that do the western democracies. Generalizing further, the time may come when on many scores totalitarian governments may do better for their populations than will the democracies. If this presents the democracies with the possibility of extinction, in the meantime it would be a not uninteresting theoretical problem to revise some traditional claims for democracy in the light of the possibility that an exploiting non-benevolent dictator may be more generous to the population than democratic leaders can afford to be.

2. Manipulation of the consumer through advertising. To say that advertising frustrates effective consumer control of the businessman, is not to say that it necessarily frustrates democratic government. But is there a connection? Hartz contends that contemporary developments have increased individuation, not submerged it; and the question can be raised both as to the importance of individuation to political democracy and as to whether advertising is one of the contemporary developments for which Hartz's hypothesis is true. The question has also been raised as to whether advertising conditions the electorate so that it can more easily be engineered, even if not by the advertisers themselves, in political affairs.

Economic theory will be of little help on this point, for economic theorists commonly employ a simplifying assumption of given wants or demands, raising no problems about where demands come from or by whom they are influenced. If this strikes a political scientist as an extraordinary defect in economics, its justification has been that the simplifying assumption is a lid on a Pandora's box.

Not only do economists thus turn their backs on the question of what manipulation might be tolerable, they do not even bother to set down the facts as to what kinds of manipulations are practiced and with what success. Voting studies as known in political science have no counterpart in economics, except in a kind of research underworld of advertisers and their staffs and a few scholars in the business schools. It is time to bring their material, which I do not mean to imply they always secrete, out into the open of academic discussion; and, if economists are prevented by an occupational habit from doing so, perhaps some students of democracy will see its relevance.

We already know, even if our knowledge is incomplete, that in many respects manipulation of consumer is like manipulation of voter. Leaders deliberately misinform and misrepresent, appeal to fears that they first arouse if not already present, and subtly strengthen some values and weaken others. On the other hand, they sometimes inform, sometimes play an important innovating role in calling attention to important neglected facts or values. Still again, in some circumstances they make appeals that divide the electorate and in other circumstances make appeals that unite them. Or they play upon desires for individuality in one case, upon desires for conformity in another.

A comparative study of political and economic manipulation of the electorate should be especially fruitful. The useful functions that a manipulating leader can perform ought not to be neglected; but, useful or not, leaders' functions in the market need investigating. In political science, top governmental leadership sometimes is represented as a passive reconciler of conflicting interests, a resultant of vectors. Sometimes, on the contrary, it is represented as itself an interest group. Still again, though less commonly, it is represented in a vigorously creative role, like that of Schumpeter's entrepreneur, formulating issues and imaginatively integrating the conflicting groups in the society who never themselves rise to leadership's level of comprehension and innovation. And where some political scientists think of leadership's function in clarifying preferences, others have suggested that for democratic consensus leadership is required to gloss over differences, muddy the perception of preferences, sometimes alter them to make them more harmonious. Some of these views are relevant to analysis of leadership in the market.

If we can find out just what kinds of manipulation are attempted and what are successful, we shall achieve gains on two fronts. The observed facts will presumably contribute to an improved theoretical formulation of the desired democratic functions of leadership, a formulation which itself should be a major objective. They will also permit us to appraise leadership's actual behavior by the more explicit and defensible standards that will be formulated. In addition to clarifying leadership's role in the market, these studies should lead to more specific formalization of governmental processes generally.

Lacking both adequate facts and well-considered standards, we are presently able to look at manipulation of the consumer and agree with both calamity howler and complacent. Again, if we judge by sufficiently high or sufficiently low standards, the present situation can be agreed to be either disastrous or happy, even where no facts are disputed. The need for sophisticated standards for judging leadership's manipulation of the electorate is therefore especially pressing.

If we do not know enough about actual practices in manipulation of the economic electorate and lack standards for judgment, we are nevertheless able to draw a great distinction between possible adverse consequences of manipulation in economy and government. Manipulation in government is sometimes a prelude to revolution, to *coup d'état*, or to the slow atrophy of competitive politics. Manipulation of consumer preferences is none of these, nor, specifically, does it seek to stir dissatisfaction with the system or put one dominant clique into power. It is a highly fragmented and competitive manipulation, seeking only to influence the consumers' "policy" choices within an unchallenged institutional framework.

It might also be argued that no other great stakes are involved in such changes in expressed consumer preferences as are effected by manipulation. What does it really matter to market democracy if I buy one kind of car rather than another or if I am induced to try to raise my prestige by serving vodka to my guests instead of whisky? Especially in a wealthy society like ours, an original choice of car or liquor is already dominated by dubious motives of conformity, prestige, display, and other hasty and frivolous considerations. Hence a manipulated preference is no less satisfactory as the basis for a market vote than an earlier one. In short, the consumer is effectively manipulated only on kinds of choices that raise no serious problems for democracy in economic life.

I rather doubt that this line of argument depreciating consumer choice is correct; but it is worth investigating, both on its own account and because it raises a larger theoretical problem about democracy. Should our normative model of democracy postulate a process in which policy responds to electoral preferences generally or only to relatively more critical preferences? One can go far, I suggest, with the argument that for many categories of preference it is not at all important that policy be responsible.

The most persuasive objection to manipulation of the consumer is not, of course, that it actually challenges democracy in market or government but that it corrupts taste and values. On the ground that to examine this thesis would take us too far afield from our concern with democracy and that it is difficult to make headway on it in brief comment, I shall not discuss it.

3. *"Nul homme sans seigneur."* Bertrand de Jouvenel has suggested that we are returning to the medieval "flight of individuals into the protection of lords" in an enlargement of the role of the corporation.[14] One aspect of this development is the rise of an expense-account elite, a group especially privileged because of their connections with business enterprise. Another is the growth around the business enterprise of services to employees, ranging from reading rooms to medical services or vacation accommodations. Still another

is the corporate demand upon executives for maximum commitment to the corporation, including the commitment to stay within the corporate staff in after-hours social and recreational activity.

What is the extent of these phenomena and what are their consequences for the social preconditions of democracy? Despite recent attention to some of them, as in *The Organization Man*,[15] we are floundering. It may be that it does not much matter for democracy, but I should think it worth knowing, for example, whether sea and air travel first class is predominantly expense account, or becoming so, and whether some categories of Manhattan restaurants are now almost wholly supported by expense accounts. For a possible threat to the preconditions of democracy, I would put even more value on examining the degree to which corporate employee services and demands for loyalty are undermining community associations. On all counts, however, we need both facts, on one hand, and criteria from democratic theory, on the other.

The expense-account and the corporate provision of services to employees can both be attacked, if we wish, through tax laws. These phenomena rise from our giving corporations tax concessions quite different from those we give a family or neighborhood association bent on providing some of these privileges or services to its own members. Sometimes the difference on tax treatment is extreme. A corporation can reduce its taxes, for example, by building a swimming pool for its employees; but, should these same persons found a swimming club and build their own pool, each member would pay a federal tax on his payments to the club. In the field of taxation alone, therefore, are a number of interesting research problems that might be freshly approached as problems in the preconditions of democracy.

The problems suggested by *nul homme sans seigneur* are staggering; and, even when we limit ourselves to problems of the preconditions of democracy, they are too many, too amorphous, too imponderable. Their analysis will make little headway until we have achieved a better understanding of the requirements for personality and small group association in a democracy. But we are so far from having achieved even that understanding, so far from knowing what empirical observations would be critical in the development of understanding, that we shall only very slowly progress.

4. Privileges of leadership. Around government leaders in a democracy are erected numerous barriers to the exercise of miscellaneous powers that fall easily into leaders' hands and that we wish them not to use. Although we are apparently willing to give high placed leaders both deference in certain limited respects and limited flattering privileges, we do draw a line. We do not permit, if we can help it, their taking a general and unspecified superior position in society. And, for specific examples, we do not want them to use their power to hire and fire for accomplishing certain private objectives, to enjoy special consideration at the hands of the police and courts, or to use their powers as buyers to win favors from those who sell to them. Presumably our attempts to restrict these high placed leaders reflect both a dislike of privilege and some fear that power is easily exploited for the purpose of winning more power.

In the case of the corporate leader, he is similarly placed to take advantage of various powers that fall to him as a member of a governing economic elite; but it appears that he is much less hedged about in using these powers. As explained above, consumer controls over business leadership can endorse or veto a product, an output, but not the methods by which the product was made. And even controls imposed from the other side of the market, by those who supply labor and other inputs, do not bear closely on details of business management. Hence, it can be argued that corporate leadership is a more personally privileged leadership than is governmental.

Not being at all confident that this is the whole story, I should like to see a comparative study of the privileges of leadership not essential to discharge of function in both government and corporation. If a significant difference is found, the next question to ask is whether it makes any difference to political democracy. At one extreme, an answer might be that we have overlooked a serious flaw in democracy in our toleration of privilege for business leaders; at the other extreme it might be discovered that our traditional fear that small powers beget large ones is unfounded. This is a line of research that responds to no generally felt public problem, but it need not be disqualified on that score. In the very long run it would throw light on, though not itself answer, such a question as one not yet seriously raised: Can we reconcile democratic aspirations with the inheritance of corporate position, as in the conspicuous case of Henry II? This is only an example of one of many possible applications.

Business influence on public policy. Business influence on the pre-conditions of democracy already having been discussed, we now ask about its influence on the political preferences of voters, legislators and other policy-makers. The subject has, however, been so much worked over that one hesitates to approach it. No doubt the business point of view on public policy is well represented in Washington, as well as in the mass media. The inevitable question is whether the competitive struggle between it and other points of view falls short of meeting any important requirement of democracy. A second question is whether reforms, such as publicly subsidized mass media, might improve the character of the competition. Important as these questions are, I shall not go over familiar ground and make instead only a few points.

In the competition of propagandas, what ought to be the limits on government propaganda to defend and implement its own policies in the face of attack by business or other propaganda? Government propaganda is often condemned by solid theoretical argument; on the other hand, presidential addresses and other public statements can hardly avoid it; and Rogow has in effect challenged traditional assumptions about the desirability of limiting it in his account of British difficulties with business propaganda.[16] Here again is a piece of the normative theory of democracy that needs working out, to which Pennock's essay makes substantial contribution.

On business propaganda itself and other business influences on policy, a distinction ought to be drawn between the twin influences of business and wealth in politics, even if the latter commonly supports the former.

Thus quite aside from the influence of money in politics, the significance of private enterprise in creating a homogeneous group of highly motivated partisans ought not to be missed. So tightly knit, so highly motivated are these partisans that Harold Laski's theses that businessmen will overthrow democratic government rather than yield on certain issues came to be widely accepted even in such relatively stable democracies as Great Britain and the United States. Although they did yield in Britain, Rogow has argued that in another sense they have not yet yielded.

The intensity of their partisan activities in the United States is nowhere better illustrated than in the doggedness with which business groups have sought to stultify the regulatory processes and capture the regulatory commissions. It has therefore been argued for the public utilities that the only way to make regulation effective in the face of partisan activities of business is to eliminate private ownership of the regulated industries. On the other hand, it has also been argued that, with the rise of a salaried managerial group in industry whose interests in and controls over their firms are not dependent upon their stock ownership, partisan activity will remain substantially the same in both private and public firms, since both business groups will take on narrow corporate goals in about the same way.

What then, a research project might ask, is the character and relative intensity of partisan political activity among owner-managers, non-owning managers of private corporations, and managers of publicly owned corporations? The findings may produce some surprises and, in any case, will throw light on some significant relations between business ownership and interest-group activity. To avoid confusing the issue, the influence of income and wealth ought to be removed from the findings; if a non-owning corporate executive is more intensely partisan than an owner-manager, we want to be sure that it is not simply because he has a higher income he wishes more intensely to protect.

A practical application of these researches would be in reconsidering regulation. But it ought not to be assumed that the less intense the partisan activity the better for democratic government. These researches would also point up the need for examining the functions performed by business partisanship, not all of which are disruptive to democratic government.

As to the influence of money in politics, inequality in income and wealth may so split a society as to make a democratic consensus impossible. But in the better established and not extremely inegalitarian societies of the western world, the problem of income and wealth in politics is that of its disproportionate influence on policy. Again, this is familiar. The threat of money is, however, presumably less serious if its influence is not linked tightly to that of a wealthy hereditary business elite. We ought to explore further, therefore, the relation between inherited wealth and membership in the business elite. It is probably just as correct to say of the United States that a man becomes rich because he is a corporate executive as to say that he becomes a corporate executive because he was born into a wealthy family. But how is business leadership recruited? Our information is fragmentary. Certainly corporations promote largely on merit, but how strong are other influences and how is merit appraised? And if corporations more solicitously woo Yale and Princeton graduates than they do the graduates of the state universities, they in effect recruit from wealth. To what extent is this the dominant pattern of recruitment?

In discussing the businessman in political office, I went into some detail on the need for explicit models of the democratic process for criteria by which the businessman's role could be appraised. In appraising the implications of the corporation for the social conditions of democracy, the need for criteria based on explicit and comprehensive theory was again apparent. Now once again, in appraising the consequences both of business partisanship and of inequality of income and wealth for the making of public policy, the need for theoretically derived criteria is no less pressing.

B. THE UNION

The consequences of the union for political democracy

are in some respects like those of business in politics. For example, questions asked about the businessman's role as a partisan, about his capacity to adopt a new role when he becomes a public official, or about his demanding an excessive organizational loyalty can all be asked again about the union leader. Similarly the need for explicit models of the democratic process by which business activity in politics can be appraised is equally apparent for the appraisal of union activity.

The leader's role in shaping attitudes. Rather than repeat in the context of unionism what has been said in the context of business, let us instead move on to still other aspects of unionism significant for democracy. It is widely agreed that the rise of unionism diminished standing disproportions in the effective representation of group interests in making and administering public policy. Unionism achieved a somewhat improved organization of the potential electoral strength of wage earners, and union leaders came to be more effective representatives in policy-making at all levels than wage earners had ever before been able to depend on. In speaking for wage-earners interests in the continued debate on public policy that goes on in newspapers, magazines, and broadcasting; in legislative lobbying; and in representation both of wage-earner and consumer interests before regulatory bodies, union leadership presumably reduced the disproportionate strength of business and wealth. Unionism has probably also raised the level of political activity and improved the "circulation of elites." All this is familiar.

As an interest group, however, organized labor is different in important respects from other groups. Compared to business as an interest group, it is more formally organized, its members' political attitudes are probably less alike in the absence of organization efforts to make them alike, its members are less confident that they know what they want in politics, and they are consequently more dependent upon advice from organization leaders. Although these hypotheses themselves need to be tested, let me suggest some implications.

It may follow from the above differences between business and labor that labor's political activity is less well characterized as a pursuit of given objectives than as a process in which objectives are themselves examined and reconsidered in the process of pursuing them. Labor's political activity, more than business political activity, is heavily influenced by a continuing interchange between leadership and rank-and-file, in which union leadership competes with other opinion leaders such as ministers, newspaper columnists, and even businessmen to whom the rank-and-file sometimes turns for advice on some issues. The competition puts leadership in a position in which it cannot depart too far from the preferences of its rank-and-file, but at the same time the rank-and file demands information and advice from leadership as to what its interests are and what its demands ought to be.

Such an interchange between leader and follower, in which the leader himself both follows and leads, is to be found in microcosm among small groups of acquaintances some of whom make a bid for opinion leadership, and is to be found again in the relation between a newspaper editor and his readers or, even if in lesser degree, in the relation, say, between businessmen and the Committee on Economic Development. It is probably nowhere more obvious than within the union movement, nor is it anywhere more highly organized on an extremely large scale than in unionism. Chains of these relationships form an intricate network when a leader of one particular union group himself turns for leadership to some one higher in the union hierarchy.

As a universal phenomenon in democratic politics that is especially vigorous and easily observable in unionism, the process ought to be systemically studied. Who communicates with whom? What is the content of the interchange? To what degree is the leader constrained in what he says and what he does in the political arena by the beliefs of his constituents? To what degree do his followers depend upon him to tell them what to believe? How is the network constructed? At what points do union leaders themselves turn to leaders outside the union movement?

These studies would add to the richness of present research on attitude formation in that they would picture not selected aspects of attitude formation but a large integrated process, in which flows of information, impact of policy problems on leaders' attitudes, competition of leaders for followers, "shopping around" of followers for leaders imposed by followers' opinion on followers, and constraints upon leaders imposed by followers' opinions would all be placed and clarified. Such studies would throw great light on a central and—I think—inadequately cultivated question: Is democracy to be construed as a political mechanism for satisfying demands of the citizenry, or is it better construed as a political mechanism for the discovering, adjusting, and only then satisfying demands of the citizenry? They would also illuminate the question imaginatively discussed in Berelson, Lazarsfeld, and McPhee:[17] In a democracy, what does the voter need to know about and what does he not need to know?

Still further, such studies would bridge a gap between some older concepts of democracy in which the voter is envisaged as choosing among policies and the newer concept in which he simply chooses among candidates, for it would somewhat clarify the relation, for different kinds of political leaders, between the leader's success in competition for leadership and his role in forming and responding to policy demands. I would also expect such studies to contribute heavily to formalization of democratic theory on these and other points. Again, Pennock's essay carries these topics further.

Fragmentation of policy-making. Conflict among interest groups has pushed political science a long way from the assumption of an objective public interest toward an appreciation of the multiplicity of publics and of interests. Although the multiplicity of interests is taken as evidence that policy will in fact finally be resolved in part by the power positions of conflicting groups, there remains in the profession a widespread feeling for an ideal in which at higher or highest levels of policy-making some kind of overview of the conflict can be had and a reconciliation achieved through a reasoned adjustment of interests. The ideal raises a problem in democratic theory that, though introduced here in connection with the union as an interest group, pertains to interest group conflict generally.

I suggest that possibilities for reconciling conflict without a

high-level overview and reasoned solution are greatly under-
valued in social and political theory, excluding only economic
theory. We in economics earn our livings theorizing about a
complex social mechanism for achieving a resolution of conflicting demands upon resources and income which accom-
plishes no central overview, no centrally determined solution,
no reasoned final reconciliation. Our pre-occupation with this
mechanism, the price system, makes us sensitive to the possibilities of achieving a high degree of coordination through
wholly fragmented decision-making. Similar possibilities of
resolving conflict and achieving social coordination through
political fragmentation, though by no means unknown to
political theory, have not been exhaustively explored. I have
myself been recently looking for counterparts in governmental processes to fragmented decision-making in the market and find the search rewarding.[18]

Again, what is required is not scattered observation of
phenomena but their comprehensive inter-linking so that the
significance of fragmentation can be seen in the light of all
the processes and requirements of democratic government.
In short and again, we need large-scale models of democracy.
And when we have them, we can deal much more surely
and precisely with the impact on democratic policy-making
of such groups as unions.

Here, of course, I tend to challenge Beer's identification of
group conflict with inefficiency in policy-making. Conflict is
of course a common source of inefficiency, but we shall mis-
understand the mechanisms of democracy if we assume this
always to be the case. That fragmented and generally dis-
jointed rather than synoptic decision-making processes can
achieve coherence as well as innovation is obscured by our
habit of defining coherence as the product of a central overview of a policy problem. In actual fact, it is clear that some
problems are too large, too complex, too imponderable to
be grasped by any one man's mind or any committee's de-
liberations. Under such circumstances a series of incremental
moves in policy achieved by mutual adjustments among shifting combinations of groups and individuals can, for all
its imperfections, often achieve coherence superior to that

achieved through a futile attempt to push the human mind beyond its limits. For it is a characteristic of such incremental mutual adjustments that they often focus attention and problem-solving capacity on such pieces of the larger problem as can be grasped, understood, and predictably controlled. And they represent also a sequential process of attending at one point to the corrections of errors—fortunately only incremental—made at other points, thus achieving a resultant coherence not through a super-human understanding beforehand but through a manageable mopping-up operation.[19]

Two kinds of coherence are, of course, not even to be desired in the real world. One is that kind of consistency in policy that is attainable only when the electorate is unanimous in its choice of values or objectives, as well as in its means or policies. I think none of us would tolerate so well ordered a society and would hope instead for the continued benefits of individual differences in values, attitudes, and proclivities. The second is a kind of consistency in which no social goal or policy is ever sacrificed for the achievement of some other. It is such a sacrifice that often prompts the complaint of incoherence, but clearly in a world in which even for like-minded people the achievement of any one of their aims is not wholly consistent with the possibility of achieving all others—where, in short, policies are costly in terms of each other—to aspire to coherence construed as "no sacrifice" is to be utopian in the worst sense.

Too much union power? If unionism has redressed a previous imbalance, it is often argued to have created a new one. If so, its excesses are not where they are alleged to be. The union in politics has not turned out to be the highly cohesive, intransigent, and intense voting bloc that was in some circles feared. Not so cohesive because of conflicts of interest among wage earners and among the allegiances within each wage earner. Not so intransigent because of two-way interchange between leaders and rank-and-file and again between policy and policy demands. Not so intense, because the wage earner is perhaps more citizen than union member. The union in the market place, however, may indeed pose a threat to economic stability; the possibilities and probabilities are much debated.

Let us assume, for the sake of argument, either that unionism in the market is disruptive or that nevertheless we wish to take steps to ensure that it never becomes so. What to do? Thinking back on Adolph Sturmthal's demonstration of more than a decade ago that organized labor behaves one way as an interest group but quite another way when it becomes responsible for the electoral success of a political party,[20] it might be argued that a desirable development in American democracy would be the assumption of party responsibility by unionism. The argument is that, once organized labor casts its lot permanently with one party rather than playing each against the other, its gains largely depend upon that party's becoming or remaining an effective competitor for the vote. Thus organized labor finds itself compelled to moderate both its political demands and its market behavior in order to find common cause with a potential electoral majority. It then finds it easier to attain its traditional segmental objectives through political means than through the market, for a potential majority can be organized around demands for social security and other welfare objectives, including income redistribution, while the pursuit of these same objectives through collective bargaining alienates the required allies. If all these hypotheses are correct, it would appear that deeper involvement of labor in the Democratic party and a consequently more predominantly political pursuit of labor's objectives might be a sufficient safeguard against excessive union demands in the market.

The hypotheses are plausible, and varying political roles of organized labor from country to country in the western world make it possible to test them by comparative analysis. Whether they are true or false, such research would add to our comprehension of the relation between interest groups and political parties, as well as clarify the processes by which potentially dangerous interest groups are curbed by their need for allies in competitive politics.

III. Private Enterprise, Price System and Regulation

Quite aside from the particular consequences of business and unionism, the structure of the economy in the large is itself consequential for political democracy. It is not, however, consequential in some of the ways traditionally alleged; and a good starting point for discussion is the consideration of two conflicting historical beliefs about economy and democracy that are in process of being reformulated.

1. It is alleged that political democracy is impossible without the private enterprise economy. Although political democracy and private enterprise arose historically in circumstances in which they appear to have supported each other, the proposition has not had to depend on this evidence alone. It has been rather persuasively argued that the market economy, removing as it does many questions from the political arena, simplifies the tasks of government, lightens the load of decision-making on political leaders, removes divisive issues from politics, minimizes the need for political authority—in all these respects easing strains on political democracy.

But the proposition fails to distinguish between the case for a price system and the case for private enterprise. Earlier the failure was unimportant, but we now know that publicly owned industries can be harnessed to a price system, and in every democracy some are now so harnessed. Today economists (whose opinions are not however conclusive on this issue) would probably largely agree that political democracy would require heavy use of a price system but would be divided on whether it required a wide scope for private enterprise.

More important, a growing number of social scientists will today declare that with the present resources of social science it cannot be known whether political democracy requires either price system or private enterprise. This I regard as a great gain, for it turns the attention of social scientists to questions of a form that can be researched and that have some relevance for the kinds of policy choices that democracies make. We now ask instead a question of the form: Will, in some specified circumstance, some specified alteration in price system, private enterprise, or government regulation be expected to strengthen or weaken democracy and, if so, in what respect? Thus we put an end to a traditional and sterile debate and turn instead to such a question as the appropriateness of public ownership for certain British industries or for certain American public utilities, or such a question as the impact of land-use planning on democracy and other values.

Pursuing this new line of questioning and suppressing the old, we find, for example, that governmentally sponsored old age insurance, unemployment compensation, and relief have almost certainly at one time or another in different countries been a major underpinning for the consensus on which democracy rests. It is therefore clear that less price system or less private enterprise and more regulation can in some circumstances be essential to democracy.

Thus our research questions in this area are best stated when they permit us, first, to take account of variety in possible relations between price system or private enterprise and political democracy and, second, when they direct us toward *incremental* changes in economic structure so that we ask about the consequences not of the price system but of *more* price system or *less,* not of government regulation but of *more* governmental regulation or *less.*

2. It is alleged that socialism is required for democracy. Assuming "socialism" to refer to the public ownership of industry, it has never been well demonstrated that socialism is required for democracy in government. Inequality of income and wealth and the power of the business leader in politics can be argued to be inconsistent with political democracy, but corresponding threats to democracy in public ownership can also be argued. Although socialism may be necessary to a highly developed democracy (and not merely by definition), the resources of social science do not permit us to know; and, again, this kind of question has generally been replaced by researchable questions that have

the additional merit of being relevant to actual policy choices open to the democracies, as illustrated in the discussion above of price system and democracy.

More often than not, this particular allegation does not specify that socialism is required for democracy in government but is to be read as claiming that economic democracy is impossible without socialism. But we have seen above that the market, even under the auspices of private enterprise or a mixture of private and public, is in many respects a democratic piece of machinery. Again, therefore, as indicated above, the relevant and researchable issues concern policy areas in which market democracy might be strengthened by specific alterations in structure, including the possibility of socialized enterprise. It is not obvious that choosing comprehensive socialist organization would strengthen economic democracy, nor do we in fact have such an option in democratic politics.

Leaving these issues aside, I finally come to a few hypotheses about economic organization and political democracy with which it seems both logically and rhetorically satisfying to bring this paper to a close. Some of these hypotheses are relevant but quite refractible to analysis; others point very directly to research.

1. *Specialization of function and the consequent hierarchical organization of skill and responsibility in all industrialized societies will appear increasingly to violate the prerequisites of political democracy.* This is a consequence both of the degree to which specialization and hierarchical development occurs and of our raising the standards for political democracy. Sooner or later, it would appear, we shall begin to be concerned with a pattern of specialization in which, say, two men make their careers out of saving time for a hierarchically superior third whom they would assist and whose talents are regarded as that much more valuable than theirs. Such a pattern is on some counts at odds with the democratic principle that one man is never the tool or instrument of another. The problem not having arisen yet with any force, we are in no position to begin research on how to solve it; but we might investigate the changing character

of superior-subordinate relations in a society of increasingly specialized functions.

2. *Many of the beliefs that have grown up around our economic system threaten the survival of a democracy in its competition, with totalitariansim.* Fiscal orthodoxy, at one extreme, and a widespread reluctance to undertake collective expenditure on science and education are illustrative. That the Soviets are drawing close to us in many fields, surpassing us in some, everyone now knows; the degree to which the state of affairs is traceable to the folklore of our economic system is less well appreciated and well worth exploring.[21]

3. *In particular, the relative inviolability of private enterprise may cripple our efforts to meet the Soviets in trade rivalry and other forms of economic warfare.* The Soviets will not be constrained by constitutional prohibition and other effective political restraints on manipulation of production, prices, investment and foreign trade. So far, no such threat has arisen, but a Soviet attempt to outrival us in trade concessions or to disorganize certain existing patterns of world trade could very quickly make it major. This is a problem worth anticipating; and it raises certain technical economic problems that can be analyzed well in advance of the need for new policy-making.

4. *To meet the above problems of rivalry with the Soviet Union, the role of government in economic life will be substantially increased.* Specifically, government activities will account for a substantially larger share of national product; collective expenditures will increase at the expense of private consumer expenditures; and government and business leadership may enter into a closer relationship in which, as in England, business associations and individual businesses take on certain functions we now think of as belonging to public administration.

5. *Democracy in local government may be strengthened by its increasing responsibilities for education, as well as for other community expenditures that will develop as we become wealthier.* This is much more a guess than an estimate of probabilities, but it suggests that we might take

a new scholarly interest in emerging patterns of community demands for collective amenities and their consequences for local government. Assuming that national democracy survives, we may soon enjoy a renaissance of local government.

Coming at the end of this essay, the above hypotheses might appear to be intended as a summary of issues. But they are not; they merely suggest research problems in one last area. Rather than attempt a summary, I shall merely point out that, of all the issues raised, the most persistently recurring have stressed the need for (1) formal comprehensive models of democracy, (2) special attention in model-building to the two-way interplay between leadership and electorate, (3) special attention also to the formalization of processes by which preferences are adjusted to each other and otherwise aggregated, and (4) reformulation of all-or-none issues into problems of incremental adjustment of institutions. Though these points constitute no summary at all, they have run like themes through much of the discussion.

Model-building, on which I have thrown so much emphasis, I see as a special form of image-building, to use Hartz's term. In his discussion of both the usefulness and the inappropriateness of images, his thoughts ran largely to those images of democratic processes that are widely held in a society and are part of the society's ideology as well as guides to conduct. A special class of images are those scholarly constructions known as models. They need not correspond to popular images, of course; nor is it even always necessary that they have ultimately some effect on lay images, for they are constructed for highly specialized analytical purposes. But just as Hartz pointed up the discrepancy between lay image and actual functioning of institutions, discrepancies between scholarly image or model and functioning have often loomed large. My repeated suggestion that students of democracy make their images formal, explicit, and precise is, of course, merely an appeal to some of the traditional aspects of the scientific method on which we count to minimize the discrepancy between the scholar's image and what can actually be observed.

Democracy and Leadership

By J. Roland Pennock
Swarthmore College

WE HAVE HAD much to say throughout this discussion of images and models. Both, I suppose, might be called "theories." By an image we generally mean a popularly held theory. Such a theory may be far removed from the facts; nor need it represent an ideal. By a model we refer to a theory or group of related theories used by scholars to describe or to aid in the understanding of (for instance) the operation of an institution or set of institutions. It may represent merely a simplified description of reality, useful for analytical purposes; or it may stand for an ideal, for a norm, for what "ought" to be. In other words, both (popular) images and (scholarly) models may be either descriptive or prescriptive.

In the case of images this distinction is often somewhat blurred, as in what Hartz calls the classical image of democracy. This image comprises a set of simple relations between atomistic individuals and sovereign states that, in the modern world at least, is neither realistic as description nor viable as norm. There is a tension between image and reality and possibility which in Hartz's opinion contributes to the anxieties of our day.

A second model (for Hartz's "image" may also be viewed as a model) has been proposed by Beer. He sees the modern democratic state as it manifests itself in Britain as a considerably collectivized polity in which individual and state are mediated by strong pressure groups and by even stronger political parties, the latter serving to produce coherence and innovation in policy that is lacking in the less disciplined American system. He sees the groups and especially the parties as the chief suppliers of leadership.

While Lindblom's forays into politics from the point of

view of an economist modestly eschew model-building, strong hints of a model may nevertheless be found in his fruitful remarks. The model he would construct (although I am sure he would not suggest it as a *complete* political model) would be built around the concept of wholly fragmented political power, using a sort of political market-place as a device for the reconciliation of interests and for achieving rational results without the existence of a central plan. If I understand him correctly this market would differ from Hartz's classical image in at least two respects: the units might be both individuals and groups; and they would act "blindly" with respect to any concept of the general interest.

In discussing the problem of leadership, I too shall deal with models and offer one of my own. For want of a better term, I shall call it "organic-pluralistic." What I mean by this concept will appear in due course. Meanwhile, let me set forth three of the more controversial conclusions of this essay, so that the reader may know what to expect and be able to see the significance of points that might not otherwise be clear at the time they are made. First, it is of the essence of the democratic ideal, as that notion has been traditionally understood, that domination should be minimized and leadership (not all leadership, but much leadership) dispersed and fragmented. Second, from the point of view of democracy as herein defined, I shall argue that what may be roughly described as the American system of government (with its checks and balances and lack of party discipline) has significant advantages over the British system. Third, this organic-pluralistic system of democracy is not rendered inherently ineffective by a weakness of leadership.

With respect to the last of the three items just mentioned, it is worth noting that it has been part of the stock-in-trade of conservative critics of democracy in all ages to assert that one of its inherent flaws is weakness of leadership. At the same time, it is frequently contended that democracy, more than other forms of government, depends upon vigorous leadership for its success. For instance, Hamilton Fyfe declares that "in a democracy everything depends on the character and ability of leaders and officials."[1] Perhaps today defenders of democracy themselves are more inclined than they have been in the past to accept the latter proposition and to harbor at last a lurking fear that there may be some truth in the first. Both of these propositions are, I believe, exaggerated. Briefly, their exaggeration grows out of the fact that they are based upon a false myth of democracy, described by Hartz, rather than upon either the democratic reality or upon the model (or myth) which it is the genius of democracy to tend toward. That is to say, they are not based upon either the democratic fact or the democratic norm properly conceived.

It may be useful in establishing the setting for this discussion to enumerate some plausible explanations for the state of mind I have described. Most obvious is the chronic international crisis that features our bipolar world and the tremendous stakes involved in atomic cold war. Perhaps it is this situation more than anything else at the present time that leads to laments over the alleged poverty of democratic leadership. From a different point of view, the contrast between the reforming spirit of the United States in the 1930s and the conformist-apathetic pattern of the postwar generation seems to many both to signal the need and to dim the prospects for stimulating leadership on the home front. Moreover, changes produced by technological developments in two ways contribute to a demand for leadership. The increased pace of change creates a need for more rapid adjustment of policies and institutions, or for what Beer calls "innovation": witness the problem of internal political boundaries created by our exploding metropolises. More broadly, as we increasingly conquer nature, it is apparent that all that stands between our desires and our satisfactions is man himself—his inertia, his conflicting demands, his irrationality.

Finally, with reference to the cry for leadership, one may speculate that the disappearance of anything like a ruling class may likewise add fuel to the demand for leaders. Perhaps there is an objective need for a substitute; or possibly there is only an irrational fear or feeling of insecurity in its absence.

II

Before going further some definitions are in order. The concept of leadership is highly amorphous. If one deals with it without careful definition and subdivision as to its kinds and dimensions, the result will almost certainly be vacuous. But once one embarks upon a more discriminating approach he risks losing both his readers and himself in a mare's nest of complexity and confusion. Seeing no escape from this hazard, in what follows I shall move from the general to the particular. More specifically, I shall begin with definitions and models, examining at this stage some "first-approximation" relations, and then explore more fully the nature and dimensions of leadership, its institutionalization, and its relations to certain American institutions, attitudes, and problems. Finally, I shall seek to place my remarks in perspective by reviewing their relations to the most relevant aspects of the contributions of other participants in this discussion.

Perhaps the simplest definition of a leader is that he is "one who influences more than he is influenced by others with whom he is associated." This definition is suggestive but too general to be adequate. Normally a leadership situation, unlike the relations between Robinson Crusoe and Friday, involves more than two people. The leader has numerous followers. Moreover, they constitute a group having a common purpose, shared with the leader. Although it may be the leader who in the first instance generates the common purpose, the relations between leader and led are thenceforth reciprocal. To be sure the leader influences more than he is influenced—at least as far as concerns his relationships with any particular individual. Indeed, in a sense he may be said to direct and control the behavior of others, although generally only within a restricted sphere, the area being determined by the nature of the shared purpose. A better way to put it perhaps is that the behavior of the leader structures or patterns the behavior of the group. He may not achieve complete integration: some members of the group may be stirred to opposition. Leadership is not the same as authority. A person whose commands are obeyed because the law so requires is not, *as such*, a leader, although the possession of authority is likely to increase a person's ability to lead.

Leadership must also be distinguished from domination. In the latter case commands are imposed, by means of force or otherwise, and the purposes to be pursued are chosen by the dominator. Moreover, persons who act in response to domination, as contrasted with followers of leaders, lack autonomy (with respect to such actions). Manipulation may be distinguished as a special type of domination. Here the patterning of behavior is achieved by more subtle psychological means than is the case with the simple dominator. Command gives way to suggestion, insinuation, conditioning, and the like. But, as with domination, the relationship is a one-way affair, and the purposes of the manipulator are imposed upon his victims. The followers of a leader accept his leadership willingly, not against their will and not automatically, that is, not as automatons. Accordingly, leadership may be defined as the influencing and directing of the conduct of others in a situation in which the followers act willingly, not automatically, and with some consciousness that the leader is acting in pursuit of purposes they all hold in common.[2]

Democracy is a term notorious for variety of definition. As a form of government it may of course be defined in formal terms, as a set of techniques. However, as the word is generally used today it denotes much more than a particular set of institutional devices; it stands for the ideal that those devices are intended to achieve or at least to approximate. For present purposes it seems proper to define it, or describe it, in a manner that emphasizes the ideal. The core of the notion is equality of primary political power among the sane adult members of the society.[3] The objective of this equality is not merely the recognition of a certain dignity of the human being as such, but it is also to provide him with the opportunity—equal to that guaranteed to others—for protecting and advancing his interests and developing his powers and personality. To the latter end devices are provided for promoting liberty and insuring equality of opportunity. Equality of condition, as contrasted with equality of opportunity, is not part of the definition. Yet to define the democratic ideal in terms of "equal eligibility to power status"[4] seems to me inadequate for present purposes; for, if as the result of such equal access we found ourselves with a society that was sharply hierarchical in accordance with inherited ability levels, I suggest that it would ill accord with the general idea of democracy. Certainly the democratic myth (including Hartz's "classical image") has carried with it the notion that equality of opportunities would tend at least to minimize differences in ability and therefore in status. Between hierarchy and democracy there is always a certain tension. It is this element of the myth that I have sought to preserve by the terms I have used and the form I have given to this preliminary model.

It follows from what has been said that the democratic ideal keeps pushing the democratic reality in the direction of equality not only of *access* to power but also of equality in the *exercise* of power. The logical limit of this process would seem to be a society in which no individual or group exercised power over others. It would be anarchy or "voluntarism," after the fashion of William Godwin. At least in any but the simplest society such a condition is unattainable. Moreover, since it would not be government but the absence of government, it would not be democracy, if that term stands for a type of government. It would, however, represent the fullest attainment of the distinctive element of the democratic ideal. This is not to say, even if we subscribe to the democratic ideal, that a government is necessarily better in proportion as it approaches the model depicted above. Writers from Aristotle to Rousseau have recognized that pure democracy is unsuited for any but the smallest societies. A democratic government must be able first of all to govern, and then attain such degree of democracy as is compatible with governing well.

It is my personal belief, as will appear, that under conditions prevailing in this country today the two ends, governing well and democracy, are compatible in marked degree. Nonetheless it must be recognized that the demands of government push in the opposite direction from any such complete equality as is visualized above, so that normally and properly the equilibrium point will be a considerable distance from what I have described as the democratic ideal. That point may come close to what we commonly mean by "liberal democracy" or "constitutional democracy."

III

Of the expressions defined above, leadership especially will require further elaboration, in terms of its types and of the various functions it performs and the processes by which it performs them. Before embarking upon this enterprise, however, it may be useful to examine schematically the relation of leadership to major governmental types, using a simple typology. This first approximation of a schema will be substantially modified at a later stage of the argument.

At one extreme, along the spectrum of societal forms, we shall place autocracy, and at the other anarchy. The latter might also be referred to as a "voluntaristic" society, a term that would emphasize its significant features from our point of view. At the first extreme, the autocrat completely dominates. Accordingly there is no need, indeed no room, for political leadership. In the impossible ideal-type at the other extreme there would likewise be no need for political leadership, or at least for any specialization with regard to this function. Not only would all adult members of the society have equal primary political power, but, through equality of opportunity and under the benign influence of self-government itself as an educating and developing contrivance (as classically set forth by John Stuart Mill), each would have attained to that knowledge of his real interests and of how to attain them that was postulated by James Mill.[5] In this situation, to repeat, there would be no necessity for leadership. All would be equally influencer and influenced. To be sure, some division of labor in political matters might be resorted to, so that, even though all might share alike in making laws, certain individuals would be charged with their administration and enforcement. But, in our model, these tasks, while they would require authority, would not entail leadership. (It will be recalled that according to our definition, the simple exercise of legal authority is not leadership.) Moreover, in accordance with is fundamental equalitarian premise, and to make assurance doubly certain in this matter of the balance of influence, the society might decide to resort to rotation in office and the device of the lot for all governmental positions.[6]

We have now established the two extreme points of a continuum along which societies may be ranged, neither of which needs or indeed admits of the phenomenon of leaders. At one end, the relationship of ruler and ruled is entirely one of domination. At the other, political relationships are essentially cooperative, although at any given time certain individuals possess authority but do not dominate. (Certain leadership functions would be performed, but by all adults, equally, at different times.) Each of these elements may be thought of as diminishing as one moves along the line until it disappears entirely at the opposite extreme. Political leadership, on the other hand, in varying degrees and of various types, exists at every point along the continuum between the pure types at the end points. In the absence of circumstances calling for different amounts of cooperative or otherwise articulated individual activities (a significant qualification), one may suppose that the amount of leadership would increase gradually from each end of the line and reach its maximum at the center point. The amounts of cooperation and of domination would vary in such a way that the total of activities coordinated by one or the other means would be constant.

We may think of the midpoint perhaps as indicating the situation in a large constitutional democracy with all the complex problems of a modern industrialized state. Here the pattern of voluntarism is most obviously unworkable; the need for leadership, other things being equal, is at its maximum. Any of a number of factors may cause an increase in the role of domination at the expense of leadership. An obvious example would be the situation where leaders fail to achieve the amount of agreement on common purposes requisite to a satisfactory or even tolerable solution to the problems confronting the nation.

Actually, this first approximation is pushing the schema too far, for numerous reasons. In the first place, the assumption that the same amounts of activities coordinated by or through the government would exist under all circumstances is unrealistic. The larger and more complex the society and the greater the sphere of governmental action, the more of such activities will be required. Consequently any one of the three factors we have been dealing with—cooperation, leadership, and domination—may vary in amount without a compensating variance in either of the others. A high degree of domination is not incompatible with a high degree of leadership.

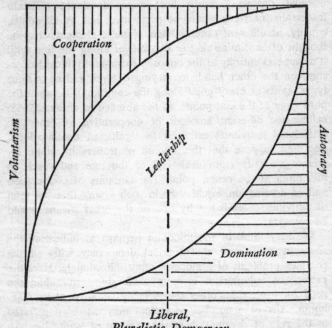

Liberal,
Pluralistic Democracy
DIAGRAM
Domination, Cooperation, and Leadership

They may even be exercised by the same person—Khrushchev, for example. Moreover, as we shall see, there are other dimensions of leadership, such as its concentration or diffusion, that are equally as important as its net amount or extent. Accordingly, any attempt to take our schema at all literally, especially in the area between the extremes, is bound to be misleading. With these warnings, however, in the accompanying diagram I attempt to portray graphically the schema I have been discussing. The total area encompassed by the rectangle represents the sum of activities coordinated by or through government.

It is implied in the foregoing remarks that it is essential to the democratic ideal that domination and autocracy should be minimized and cooperation maximized. Under the conditions prevailing in the great states of today any democratic government will have great need for leadership of all kinds; but, even here, *other things being equal,* the more fully a democracy realizes its ideal-type, or approaches its limit, the *less* need there will be for leadership.

At this point it is necessary to guard against misunderstanding by insisting that, in speaking of democracy's "ideal-type" or "limit," I refer to what is designated on the diagram as a "voluntaristic society," not to "liberal democracy." It is not meant that for any likely political situation such an arrangement would be practicable or ideal. What I am arguing is that a *bias* away from domination and toward cooperation is implicit in the notion of democracy; for to democracy the fullest possible development of the individual is of central importance. It remains true that most democracies today need more and better leadership; but especially they need *dispersed* leadership, more and better "little" leaders.

Theorists of democracy by no means always approve or recognize this bias. They have often accepted essentially elitist premises, much closer to the autocratic than the voluntaristic pole, an autocratic theory of leaders and masses, or, to use the terms of Daniel Bell, of "mindless-masses" and "strong-willed leaders."[7]

The extent to which John Stuart Mill relied on his faith that the masses would follow the leadership of their betters is well known. A similar assumption underlies the classical theory of parliamentary government to the effect that the legislative body does no more than say "yes" or "no" to the proposals submitted to it by the Government. In the United States, Henry Jones Ford and many others have set forth this theory as the model to which American government should aspire, or at least as the standard by which it should be judged. Today Mr. Walter Lippmann declares: "The executive is the active power in the state, the asking and the proposing power. The representative assembly is the consenting power, the petitioning, the approving and the criticizing, the accepting and the refusing power."[8] And in England John Plamenatz remarks that "it has always been widely admitted, though not by everyone, that the role of the people in government is negative."[9]

The overtones, indeed the implications, of all these statements are suggestive of a type of leadership that is heavily tinged with domination. This is not to say they are wrong. Probably without this theory and practice democracy would have been completely unworkable in Nineteenth century England. Nor is it likely that anything approaching the opposite extreme is likely to develop or that it would be feasible. But it may be suggested that the *tendency* is in the opposite direction—even in England. Perhaps even now the waning of class politics is sounding the death knell of the old theory. One may even speculate that the current hints of revival in the Liberal party (whether or not that revival materializes) may be one symptom of the passage of the conditions necessary to the effective operation of what we may call autocratic or elitist democracy, while Labor's recurring internal travails may point in the same direction. More significantly the widely noted growth of pressure group politics in England threatens the demise of political duopoly.

Another kind of democratic theory, while not relying upon domination-tinctured leadership, tends to neglect the whole problem of leadership, not even assuming what would be necessary for a quite simple democratic society. According to this theory, which we may roughly associate with the names of Bentham and James Mill and of the British Radicals, not to mention Andrew Jackson or Jean-Jacques Rousseau, the people should rule. A modest education for all would be enough to enable each to know his own interest and to see how to exercise the franchise so as to maximize that interest. This notion approximates Hartz's "classical image" of democracy.[10] It may be thought that this simple-minded theory of democracy is no longer held in educated circles; but this would be dismissing the matter too easily. For instance, some defenders of democracy against the criticism that it is ineffective or inefficient quickly and (to my way of thinking) mistakenly concede the point and reply by contending that democracy is interested in freedom or equality rather than effectiveness, without forcing an examination of the extent to which leadership may enable us to have our cake and eat it too.[11] Moreover, and perhaps more to the point, modern group-equilibrium theory may tend to make the same assumptions, or lack of assumptions, as characterized radical democratic theory. Just as Rousseau assumed that the errors of individual wills would cancel one another out and so allow the General Will to prevail, and as Bentham too easily accepted the doctrine of the Unseen Hand in his faith that the summation of special interests would be identical with the general interest, so much of modern group theory accepts the same principle with nothing more than the substitution of groups for individuals.[12]

This type of theory and the institutions it breeds tends to lead to the politics of logrolling and stalemate. Often of course it does not. I am not saying that a pluralistic society cannot operate democratic institutions satisfactorily. I would contend for precisely the opposite proposition. My point is simply that for a group society to work in democratic fashion more is needed than an automatic cancelling of opposing interests.

IV

Democracy, as I understand it, cannot rely (certainly not solely) on elitist democratic theory nor on Hartz's "classical image," nor on what may be termed "radical-democratic" theory. Elitist theory is unsatisfactory as a norm for democracy because it is too patronizing. It makes too little allowance for human dignity. It relies too heavily upon hierarchy. Under many circumstances it may represent a realistic pattern of what happens, and even of the best that can be expected; but as an ideal of what is to be striven for it must always remain inadequate from the point of view of democratic goals. If it is part of the function of a political theory to hold up a standard, it fails by that test. The classical image, as Hartz points out, is unrealistic not only in the oversimplicity of its individual-state dichotomy, but also in its rationalistic, or, better, intellectualistic assumptions. It not only fails to correspond to reality; it is so far removed from what today seems possible or even desirable that it fails also as a useful ideal. What I have termed "radical-democratic" theory is closely related to, if not identical with Hartz's "classical image," and so is subject to the same strictures. I may add here that it is too individualistic. It tends to *anomie,* to a situation in which cooperation, domination, and leadership are all lacking. The individual who is supposed to be the heart and soul of democracy must himself be sparked with spirit; and today we know that one requisite of such spirit is a healthy group-life.

The last sentence gives the clue to what is missing from all the theories we have just enumerated. It is the group—the element the pluralists sought rightly but without complete success to fit into a viable democratic theory. They supplied a necessary "organizing idea" that was missing from the classical theorists. But more than this idea, and more than the political parties, the pressure groups, the unions and the churches, for which that idea found a place, more than all of these, I suggest, was overlooked by classical theory. That was so concerned with the role of groups in the state that it gave insufficient attention to what goes on *within* the group. Democracy's problem, it is often argued, is the control of elites. In large measure it is. But, more than that it is the use of the members of elites in all kinds of organizations and informal groups in such a way that they generate a flow of ideas, sentiments, loyalties, and knowledge that moves up as well as down. A theory or model that gives adequate attention to this side of the picture, I believe, can serve democracy at the present stage better than any other. It is more accurate as description and more useful as prescription.

The theory I am referring to is by no means new or original.[13] It is set forth here not as a discovery but merely to indicate its relationship to the problem at hand. It lays emphasis on groups and on the group-process; but the accent is on what goes on *within* the groups rather than on the relationship of group to group. It stresses discussion rather than consent and voting. It is keenly aware of the need for continuous intercommunication both of ideas and feelings, and in stressing the latter it helps correct the over-intellectualism of radical-democratic theory. It realizes that this process must go on at all levels, from top to bottom, and make use of all sorts of media and organizations, non-political as well as political. It not only insists that the communication must be a two-way process but it also holds that the process must be shot through with mutuality. In any full statement of it, words like "feedback" and "integrate" come in for tiresome reiteration. But such processes are neither started nor continued without leadership—leadership in practically every cell and every significant substructure of the whole complex organization. I almost said "organism." Perhaps to introduce that dangerous word is to invite trouble, not to say misunderstanding. Yet it is tempting to remark that perhaps individualism, in any but the most elementary sense, is less essential to democratic theory than has been widely thought. A kind of organism ("softened by a 'quasi' ") may be democratic rather than autocratic, Hans Kelsen, T. D. Weldon, and others to the contrary notwithstanding.[14] Indeed, it is within the group, through this quasi-organic group process, that the responsible individual can attain his fullest development. And responsible government, in the fullest sense of that term, must rest on responsible citizens. For lack of a better term, we may call this the "organic-pluralistic" theory of democracy, and add it to the models introduced at the outset.

As I have indicated, the group-process that is so central to "organic-pluralistic" theory is normally dependent upon and infused with leadership. Indeed, I suggest, it is increasingly by way of the reciprocal influences of leader and led in all sorts of groups and organizations that coherence (in the sense of consistency of policy) is to be obtained in a democracy. As electorates become more informed and less willing to follow the lead of their "betters," the older devices for achieving coherent policies become less effective. Elitist democracy works less well or becomes less elitist. Popular demands that may be mutually inconsistent tend to break through the dikes of party discipline and effectively assert themselves at the policy level. Alternatively, the parties, anticipating such developments, preserve discipline by yielding to pressures that entail departures from the standard of coherence. Leadership, operating through the group process, provides no panacea for this problem. But it does provide an important means for combining individual self-expression and self-development with rational adjustment of conflicting interests willingly accepted. In other words, with the development of organic-pluralism, it becomes increasingly necessary and also increasingly possible to achieve a measure of rationality and coherence at lower levels than is assumed by elitist theory or is possible with a less participant public.

V

It now becomes necessary to elaborate somewhat on the nature of leadership, as it has been defined in this essay. What functions does a leader perform? And how, at least in a general way, does he perform them?

Let me suggest that there are four main functions. First there is the role of aiding the thought of others. Partly this is simply a matter of identifying and pointing out problems for which political action is appropriate. The problems may already be in existence in the sense that the public welfare is in some respect suffering, or its improvement being hampered; or the leader may be anticipating problems. Having noted the rising birthrate, he points out that school facilities, adequate once, will be woefully wanting in a few years. At this level, and in the case of other, more subtle, examples of anticipation, there is more need for a leader to identify problems than when the matter has already become obvious. Next in the process of aiding the thought of others comes the stage of analyzing the problems, of seeking causes, identifying the most likely points and means of attack, of calculating the probable effects of various possible courses of action, of showing what values are involved in each case, and by insightful and dramatic presentation, of helping individuals to weigh these values and to reach judgments that are sound from the point of view of their own interests.

The second function of leadership, once people's opinions are formulated, is that of enabling them to be effective. The leader provides goals, sets of ideals, to the support of which like-minded people can rally. He is a standard bearer. He provides a flag around which followers can gather, unite, and organize for effective action. He also supplies a tongue with which to articulate their views. He is indeed their representative. And if it is true that no one can completely represent another, it is equally true that for particular purposes—and they may be very broad purposes—a skillful leader may present the interests and views of someone else far more effectively than that person could do it for himself. Finally, he proposes a plan of action.

Thus far we may have many leaders, each with his own band of followers, marching off in as many different directions. The third task of leadership is to obtain the agreement of an effective combination on a single policy in each problem area, and on an order of priorities among different problems. Assuming a lack of such agreement in the first place, it is clear that minds and wills are going to have to be changed. Here the leader must both initiate and facilitate changes in group purposes. He may modify the purpose of his own group. He may persuade other leaders to alter their purposes and those of their followers. Or he may appeal directly to the followers of other leaders to gain their support for the objectives of his group or at least to make them more ready to accept some modification of their original goal. Better yet —and this is as applicable to in-group as out-group leadership—he may discover and suggest means for integrating apparently contradictory purposes. All the arts of persuasion combine with intellectual analysis to aid the leader in this role. A great capacity for empathy is an incomparable asset to this kind of leadership. Even beyond this, a combination of qualities that characterize the most spectacular leaders defies analysis: hence we call it "charisma."

Finally, even after a large area of agreement is attained, it remains to get it translated into action. For this more than assent, and more even than will is required: the will must be strong; there must be energetic determination. This fourth task of energizing his followers is by no means the least important of the leader's functions. To be sure, the extent to which even the most talented leader is likely to succeed in accomplishing either this or the preceding functions will depend on other factors than those that are personal to him. Specifically, it will be a consequence of the extent to which human impulses are being thwarted. But, granted the evidence of such thwarting, leaders will differ greatly in their ability both to canalize and to energize the latent potential.[15] Here their dramatic ability, their capacity to appeal to basic emotions, their understanding of the values held by their would-be followers, and their own infectious enthusiasm and self-confidence (the latter to convince followers that inspiring goals are attainable) will be important among the factors determining their success.

A particular leader may concentrate his efforts on some one or two of these functions, a point that will be developed more fully later on. Moreover, the first, especially, might almost be said to be ancillary rather than central to leadership *per se.* It is most easily delegated or its results borrowed from persons we would not normally think of as leaders. The identification or even solution of problems may be carried out by obscure scholars, for example, whose efforts would bear no fruit unless picked up by others. In other words it is essential to leadership that this function be performed, but it need not be performed by the leader himself and unless it is combined with other functions of leadership it could hardly be said to be a part of leadership.

With respect to all that has been said above about the nature of leadership it must be remembered that the true leader will be the object of influence as well as its subject. Doubtless leaders vary tremendously in this respect. Some seem to do little more than select and magnify the feelings of the crowd. Obviously, however, a leader who performs all of the functions enumerated above will do much more than this. On the other hand, if he is to avoid domination, he must be a receiver as well as a giver. Not only will he be influenced by people as he finds them, but also he will inspire and enable them to become greater sources of influence—on him and on others.

In discussing leadership, then, we are dealing with a very complicated phenomenon. It has many dimensions. For instance, one may attempt some measurement of the *extent* of leadership—in a given society, or, more practically, in a given situation. How much is one person influencing others? It is obvious, however, that the way in which leadership shades off into manipulation or domination means that any such measurement will be extremely difficult and at best a crude approximation.

Fully as significant is the *distribution* of leadership. At any given time, at the extreme, all political leadership may be concentrated in one man ("big" leadership.) More characteristically it may be widely distributed, both vertically and horizontally, functionally (that is, by specific type of interest) or on a geographical or other basis. A widely dispersed leadership pattern ("little" leadership), may or may not be pyramidal in form. The pattern of leadership and the persons in whom it chiefly resides may remain constant over fairly long periods of time, or it may be subject to frequent changes. Leadership may also be variously distributed as between those having official governmental capacity and those who do not (unofficial leadership). Likewise, leadership may be highly institutionalized or it may be purely personal. And this distinction does not necessarily follow that of official *versus* unofficial.

Simplifying slightly the account given above of the nature of leadership, it may be said that acts of leadership may be classified as to whether they are initiating, coordinating, or energizing. Another dimension of the subject relates to the levels at which the leadership in question is operating. Or, if we are considering a society as a whole or in its political aspects, it has to do with the distribution of leadership among these levels.

Leadership types may be classified in various ways. An obvious possibility is to categorize them in terms of the relative emphasis they place on each of the three types of leadership acts just enumerated. Thus there is the initiating leader, the innovator. The name of Franklin D. Roosevelt quickly suggests itself as an example. Other leaders play their major role in coordinating the desires and efforts of others so that they are mutually consistent. There are various ways of achieving coordination. At the lowest level it may be by the simple process of trading, the art of political brokerage. Or in more subtle and refined fashion a leader, Clement Attlee for instance, may build an administrative organization that aids in channeling disparate demands in ways that produce harmony. In addition to the initiator and the coordinator there is the energizer. Both Franklin Roosevelt and Sir Winston Churchill qualify for this category, but like all *great* political leaders they were outstanding in more ways than one. In the case of the energizer, the ideas may not be his; he may have no real claim to initiation; but he "puts them across" by arousing, exciting, inspiring great numbers of people. He may get the ideas from the people themselves, picking up a strand of common discontent or longing and showing his followers how to have their way. Such a leader may be acting democratically; he may also become a demagogue. On the other hand he may impose upon large numbers of people his own ideas or those of some other individual. By the sheer force of his personality he may virtually compel them to follow a course of action that is, let us say, both against their real interests and against their own better judgment. Insofar as such a "crowd-compeller" succeeds in this fashion he is really more dominator than leader as those terms are used in this chapter. Finally, it may be noted that problem-solving may be used by all three types (whether performed by themselves or by someone else for them), but especially by the first two.

Many other bases for classifying leadership types have been suggested. Much that has been said up to this point suggests that leadership plays an innovative or at least a dynamic role; but it is not necessarily so. It may also be conservative. Nor does this category embrace only the leader who actively organizes opposition to an innovative leader. More distinctively, conservative leadership may be primarily symbolic. Such a leader may achieve his conserving purposes by seeming to embody and symbolize the values for which the *status quo,* or something closely approximating it, stands in the minds of large numbers of people. Among recent American Presidents, "Silent Cal" Coolidge—who emitted more words for the record, per year, than any previous President—provides perhaps the clearest example of this type of leadership.[16]

Finally, it may contribute further to an understanding of the complexity of leadership phenomena to suggest one other basis of classification. Some leaders are "extremists." They adopt a position far from the mode of existing attitudes and unyieldingly seek to gain support for it and will settle for nothing less. A second type have definite policy views which they seek to have carried out, but they are willing to compromise, if necessary, as the price of some degree of success. They may be denominated "agitational" leaders. Finally, there are the "facilitative" leaders, who are neutral as to policy and whose concern it is simply to get agreement on something, to remove the source of conflict.[17]

VI

In view of the vast variety of functions that leaders must perform, even granted that they need not necessarily be combined in the same persons, it is virtually inevitable that in today's immense and complicated societies leadership should be institutionalized. This means not only that there are certain settled expectations as to the modes of behavior and the jobs to be performed by people in certain situations, but also that large staffs are built up to aid the leader in playing his role. Obviously certain types of leadership activity, or at least preparation for them, are more easily delegated than others. But even those that are intensely personal can be greatly facilitated by staff work that builds up a certain image of the leader's personality. The most obvious example of institutionalized political leadership is the American presidency. There is no need to detail here the ways in which the Executive Office of the President, twelve-hundred strong, provides the raw materials and creates the environment for leadership.[18] Of course a great deal still depends upon the capacities and inclinations of the President himself; but to an ever-increasing extent the Presidency has been built up to a point—partly by the device of institutionalization and partly because of the expectations created by the actions of past Presidents and especially their use of the newer mass media —from which retreat is virtually impossible. As Elmer Cornwell puts it, "While in the nineteenth century the man made the office over in his image, in the twentieth, more and more, the giant public image of the office will mold the man to its demands."[19]

In the Office of the President we simply see writ large what on a smaller scale is happening on all sides. Of course there was a sense in which Franklin Roosevelt was his own Secretary of State. Moreover, under President Eisenhower, John Foster Dulles made minimal use of the staff facilities of the State Department. But the self-sufficient, lone wolf role that he achieved in that office is not likely to be matched or even approached in the near future. Moreover, his critics maintained that he provided an excellent negative demonstration of the need of foreign policy leaders for staff assistance for their leadership functions. In Congress, too, the same process is in full swing, with staffs for Majority and Minority leaders, for committee chairmen (and ranking minority members) and for individual Congressmen. Nor is it only official leadership that seeks this kind of implementation. The same device is used by all kinds of private organizations, whether it be the Council on Foreign Relations, the National Planning Association, the Committee for Economic Development, the National Council of Churches, the AFL-CIO, the American Farm Bureau Federation, or the United States Chamber of Commerce. Of ever-increasing importance in this category are the private foundations. Indeed they play a rather distinctive role in that they seek to lead especially by discovering, stimulating, and encouraging leaders outside of their own organization. Here the search for leadership, innovative leadership in particular, has been itself institutionalized.

Doubtless the institutionalization of official leadership, inevitable though it is, has its dangers. The leader's staff may become more of an obstacle than an aid. Parkinson's Law contains more than a modicum of truth, and there is no reason to believe that it is confined to the "line" side of bureaucratic structures. Whenever it becomes necessary—or is thought necessary—to "clear" each move through innumerable staff members dry rot has begun to set in. Resultant delays, at best, are likely to spoil the timing of leadership moves. Spontaneity is lost; character and personality are smudged.

It would be wrong to assume that such costs represent the necessary price of leadership on the grand scale in modern society. On the contrary there is here an important area for research. We need studies of the institutionalization of leadership in various contexts and at various levels, executive, legislative, and in party organizations. What can such institutionalization at best accomplish? How well is it in fact doing the job? What are the effects on the leader? On his relations with his followers and with other leaders and their followers? Does it have an effect on the type of person who tends to be selected for leadership offices?

VII

Not all that has been said in the preceding pages about the nature and dimensions of leadership and concerning its institutionalization in large modern states provides bases for distinctions between leadership in a democracy and leadership in any other kind of polity. But most of it does. For instance, among the functions of leadership enumerated above, democratic leadership especially must develop the first—aiding the thought of the people by identifying and analyzing problems and showing the consequences of various possible courses of action in terms of popular values; and almost equally the second—enabling people to make their opinions effective. In the case of the third function—getting widespread agreement on policy—the nature of democracy demands that to the greatest extent possible this end be obtained by interaction. The emphasis, that is to say, is on the kind of leadership that involves the maximum of give-and-take between leader and led. Just as leadership is to be preferred to domination, so, within the broad ambit of leadership, that which is farthest from charismatic leadership most nearly approaches the democratic ideal. This means more emphasis on the intellectual or rational approach stressed in the classical democratic image, and less on the emotional. It also means that the leader will be more open to being influenced by those whom he is leading; and not just influenced out of considerations of immediate self-interest, but also and especially by gaining new insights in the process of interaction. It follows from what has just been said that democratic leadership tends to be widely distributed in all of the ways suggested above.

Finally, with respect to institutionalization of leadership, democracy may impose what superficially look like opposing demands. The point just made indicates that it is vital for leaders and led in a democracy to have a great deal of direct personal contact. On the other hand, the leader's staff members may get between him and his public. But this need not be so. If staffs operate as they should, they will aid rather than interfere with the objective of maximizing direct personal contact between leader and followers.

VIII

The foregoing discussion should provide the foundation for a thorough examination of any particular set of democratic institutions. Clearly no more than a few hints at what such an inquiry might disclose can be attempted here. In the pages that follow I shall give a cursory glance at our leading institutions from this point of view and also have my say— everyone is doing it—as to the significance for present purposes of what David Riesman calls our prevailing "otherdirected" temper.

In a general way the practical implications of the theory of the role of leadership in a modern, Western democracy have already been adumbrated. It calls for a loosely integrated and highly pluralistic society with the maximum opportunity for the performance of leadership functions, of one kind or another, at virtually every pore. Not only opportunity but actualization. What about specifically political institutions? Does our analysis throw any light on the relative preferability, *from the point of view of the democratic model,* of a parliamentary (majoritarian) or a presidential (check-and-balance) system? The former facilitates the formation of majorities and places the fewest obstacles in the way of their working their will, while the latter relies more heavily upon what is sometimes called "the politics of adjustment" and upon what Lindblom describes as reconciliation of conflicts without "high-level overview." It is common to think of the majoritarian system as more democratic. The equalitarian premise of democracy calls, so runs the argument, for the simplest and surest method for letting the majority have its way. By the same token, according to the usual manner of thinking, the presidential, or American system must be defended, if it is to be defended at all, on the ground that democracy needs to be curbed. Our analysis of democratic leadership, however, appears to point to the opposite conclusions. If we accept the "developmental" concept of democracy postulated in this essay, and the organic-pluralistic model, we should seek dispersed leadership, the substitution of "little" leadership for "big" leadership, wherever it can be done successfully. Not only is democratic leadership more dispersed but also its nature changes. More emphasis is placed upon the intellect as its tool and less on appeals to emotions. This directive, too, calls for close contact and small group operations. Moreover, the lieutenant leaders in such a system, since to be democratic leaders they must be open to influence as well as influencing, must have a maximum of independence, not subject to the discipline of the top command. It is of course no accident that totalitarian "leaders" everywhere oppose those independent groups that are like "worms within the entrails of the state," in Hobbes' phrase. Nor is it because they may become conspiratorial revolutionary societies. Rather, they recognize them as the heart of the democratic system to which they are opposed. It would appear then that democratic leadership calls for the kind of loose and relatively undisciplined party system that tends to go with the dispersion of power characteristic of checks and balances. Obviously federalism, not least because of its effect upon the party system, makes in the same direction.

Since conclusions contrary to the position I am here developing are so widely accepted even by those who reject the majoritarian corollary, it may be worth while to approach the matter from another angle. Why is it so widely believed that simple majority rule, in the sense of translating into action the will of fifty percent plus one of the adult population as quickly as possible, is required by democracy's fundamental principle, equality? The ideal of such a system, I suggest, is unanimity (and short of that, "government by consent," as that phrase is used by Lindblom). The intellectual founders of modern democracy never held otherwise. For Locke, the majority principle was a matter of convenience. In the absence of agreement upon any other number, the consent of the majority "passes for that of the whole."[20] And Rousseau, generally thought of as the father of majoritarian and even plebiscitary democracy, believed that the will of all would be most likely to express the general will when it approached unanimity, and stipulated that no action should be taken on the more important questions without the concurrence of extraordinary majorities.[21] Moreover, unanimity is the ideal sought by small groups, starting with the family. Committees, faculties, and similar organizations endeavor to find the widest possible bases of unity before taking action, especially if the action is vigorously opposed by a minority. Under certain circumstances, moreover, decision by a bare majority may not be the best way to achieve substantial equality of power even when the requirement of a special majority is not feasible. A group of nine people, let us say, is engaged in some continuing enterprise requiring cooperative action and periodic decisions on a particular point about which it is sharply and consistently divided. Five prefer to perform the task by method A (perhaps involving a pleasant walk by the seashore); four prefer method B (using a short, less esthetically pleasing route, but saving time). The majority principle could hardly in any substantial sense be said to answer the dictates of equality. Both fairness and equal treatment would call for allowing the four to have their way some of the time.

The example just discussed is not meant to suggest that the Speaker of the House of Representatives should occasionally declare that the Ayes have it when in fact the count revealed that the Noes were in the majority. But it is meant to give pause to doctrinaire applications of the majority principle as the epitome of democracy, and to agree with Lindblom in suggesting that the reconciliation of conflict (and achievement of coherence) by means of fragmented decision-making is an important democratic device often neglected by political theorists.[22] It may also be remarked parenthetically that Mr. Anthony Downs's analysis of the basic logic of government decision-making shows that even in the parliamentary type of democracy, assuming completely logical behavior, majority rule will not necessarily prevail.[23] Whether what *will* prevail would be more or less in accord with the principles underlying this paper is not clear without further analysis. Nor does Downs even attempt to apply his reasoning to a complicated constitutional system like our own. I mention these points only to indicate the need for further theoretical investigation in this area.

There is still another reason why democracy calls for dispersed leadership. If we accept the Millean principle that a major argument for adopting democratic institutions follows from the developmental effect on the citizens of political participation, then the institutions should be such as to encourage more than a mere choice of leaders and the rather unrealistic debates that grow out of a situation where the alternatives are always sharply structured. To be sure, too great fragmentation of the decision-making process may defeat this particular purpose. Whether or not Lindblom's suggestion that such policy determination, without "overview," may be an effective device for reconciling conflicts is correct, we must remember that as long as important policies are to be made centrally (and it would be hard to imagine the contrary) not all leadership can or should be dispersed. Moreover, competition for central leadership positions—in the form of electoral campaigns—will play a most valuable educational and developmental role.

In contrast to Lindblom and the approach suggested here, Beer takes a somewhat different point of view. He likes the greater power of British party leaders. Apparently he sees here no threat of antidemocratic "domination," or of elitist control. Or if he sees such a tendency he does not consider it a "threat." He welcomes the "coherence" and "innovation" he believes it gives to British policy, and deplores the "inefficiency" of American policy. I shall limit myself to two observations in this connection. In the first place, with respect to trends, as Beer himself notes, there are signs of pluralistic developments threatening the party duopoly in Britain. He concedes that the increase of state intervention in the economic system has led to greater participation by interest groups in the policy-making process and has forced greater dependence upon their consent. He also admits the possibility that the use of public relations campaigns by pressure groups may be on the increase. My own observation leads me to believe that he is right in both instances, that these trends are likely to continue, and that they must inevitably tend to weaken the power of the political parties, and especially of the party leaders. As this happens I would anticipate a decline in the coherence of party programs.

My second point relates to a question as to what are the facts of the case. We are in agreement that coherence of policy (in some sense at least) is desirable. Beer believes that centralized power means that there is a greater chance for deliberate, innovative, and coherent solution, while the vice of the American system of fragmented and dispersed power is inefficiency. If true, these propositions are certainly significant, although not necessarily determinative. How can they be tested? It is sometimes thought to be self-evident that central direction must be more rational in its results than a system making great use of dispersed, partly independent decisions; but Lindblom (in my view) rightly argues that this need not be so. Are centrally fixed prices necessarily more rational (in terms of the allocation of resources they produce) than those resulting from the higgling of a competitive market? May not political decision-making, within certain limits, operate in a fashion analogous to that of the market? And, I would add, may this not tend especially to be true if there is abundant opportunity for the operation of relatively independent leadership within groups at all levels?

Moreover, the comparison of policies and programs with respect to coherence is no easy matter. Is it clear that the United States is so inferior to Britain in this respect? The evidence seems to me to be lacking. It may be noted in passing that examples of what appears to be incoherence sometimes disappear on closer examination. The American system of tariffs supplemented by financial aid to foreign governments is not necessarily an example of incoherence. The two by no means completely defeat each other. Nor is it self-evident that the net effect of the two is in any sense irrational. Incidentally, too, the British combination of agricultural subsidies with Dominion preference might be attacked on similar grounds. More fundamentally, perhaps, it should be pointed out that coherence is a test that should be applied vertically over time as well as horizontally. Whatever British policies gain during a given Government's tenure of office they may lose at the next general election. Switches from private to public ownership and then again to private in the cases of steel and road transport may be cited as examples. If the programs of American major parties tend to be somewhat more alike than is the case with their British counterparts, as is widely believed to be so, this should make for greater coherence of legislative and administrative action in the United States, in the long run. Furthermore, it is more than possible that this greater degree of agreement or consensus in this country reflects the results of dispersed "little" leadership, operating at all levels and in all sorts of groups, as contrasted with the more centralized British system.

One final caveat under this heading. All that has been said is based upon the assumption that I am speaking of what is democratic—not of what is necessarily good. Alternatively, it presupposes the existence of conditions that will enable the pluralistic system we have been discussing to achieve a reasonably satisfactory solution of the country's problems. If this system does not result in sufficient agreement for action to be taken, or if it does not call forth ideas equal to the tasks that are faced, the whole situation is changed. Under such circumstances of crisis it is to be hoped that "big" leadership, even charismatic leadership, will take over where the other variety has failed. That it has generally done so in the past may be more than an accident and yet less than a guarantee that it will always do so in the future. This is not a counsel of either irresponsibility or despair. The more closely a democracy approaches its ideal-type the less need there is for big leadership and the less willingness to accept it. Conversely, when the need is there, when human impulses are being seriously frustrated on a wide front, the temper changes. It is not that such circumstances magically bring forth leadership equal to the occasion; but it does appear to be true, and in accord with well known phenomena of social psychology, that people in deep trouble select and listen to leaders who have conviction, determination, the ability to sense the needs of the situation, and other leadership qualities demanded. Indeed it may be suspected that charisma is as much a product of the situation and of the followers as it is an independent personal quality.[24]

IX

Turning to a necessarily sketchy discussion of certain particular institutions of American democracy in the light of what has been said up to this point, the Presidency demands first attention. Here it is not a question of explaining the importance of dispersed leadership. Rather, we are here dealing with the primary American institution for centralized power, overview, and focus for popular attention on national policy. Division of power requires a counter-poise, and dispersed leadership needs a focal point and indeed a climax. The eminence and uniqueness of the President's position assures him an almost unequaled leverage for leadership. His constitutional and political powers are great. It is arguable of course that they are not great enough. But it cannot be denied that they are very great indeed if, as Max Lerner puts it, "he has grasp, contagion, political artistry, and a mastery of his purposes and methods. . . ."[25] It is true, too, as Lerner also declares, that even the strongest President "is helpless except insofar as he can win the people's confidence."[26] Significantly, Lerner attributes this fact not to the separation of powers or other constitutional limitation but to certain characteristics of the American people, especially a general skepticism of political power and an emphasis on individual self-reliance which, whatever its origin, is today nurtured and reinforced in the American pattern of family life and by our school system.

It is sometimes felt that the job is too big for any man, or at least for any but the rarest of Presidents. But could more men—for example, a cabinet system—do it better? Could they, for instance, keep a closer eye on all significant aspects of national policy and keep it unified, coherent? Here I can do no more by way of answering that question than to express strong doubts and cite one wisp of supporting evidence. L. S. Amery, member of several British cabinets, has criticized that institution, even as it operates with a secretariat, for failure to coordinate departmental policies. "There is very little cabinet policy, as such," he declares, "on any subject. No one has time to discuss it, to coordinate its various elements or to see to its prompt and consistent enforcement. There are only departmental policies."[27] The major job of coordination is done in England by the Prime Minister and two or three others. Much the same—substituting the President for the Prime Minister—can be said for this country, although President Eisenhower made strenuous efforts, with some success, to achieve "team" policies.

One other aspect of the Presidency calls for brief discussion: selection. Ever since Lord Bryce wrote his famous chapter on "Why Great Men Are Not Chosen Presidents," numerous students of politics have lamented this same alleged fact. To cite Max Lerner once more, he maintains that "the conditions for reaching the Presidency are so haphazard and opportunist that the way is too often open for a genial mediocre man who means well, commands a popular following, and will not be too intractable."[28] It can hardly be denied that mediocre men have not infrequently been elected to the Presidency. But, if the implication is that the British system does it better, a glance at the record will raise some doubts. Since the turn of the century we have had McKinley, Theodore Roosevelt, Taft, Wilson, Harding, Coolidge, Hoover, Franklin D. Roosevelt, Truman, Eisenhower, and Kennedy. For the same period the roll of English Prime Ministers ran as follows: Balfour, Campbell-Bannerman, Asquith, Lloyd George, Bonar Law, Baldwin, MacDonald, Chamberlain, Churchill, Attlee, Eden, and MacMillan. Can it be said with any assurance that the latter list includes more "great leaders" or a greater sum total of leadership ability than the former?

It is true that there are aspects of our selection system that one might expect to militate against the selection of outstanding men. One thinks particularly of the operation of the electoral college. It does eliminate from serious consideration many men who might become—and sometimes men who already are, in their own states—effective leaders. By dampening if not completely eliminating the contest in many states, it certainly does anything but provide incentive for leadership experience in those states. The pros and cons of the numerous plans for revision that have been advanced are entirely too complicated for consideration here. Although Ruth Silva[29] and other critics of revision have given me pause, I am not completely convinced that it is impossible to work out a plan that would remove the major disadvantages of the present system without letting us in for other evils equally great.

Of Congress, perhaps the most general remark that can be made is that the substantial differences between the Senate and the House provide the beginning of one of the avenues down the line from big to little leadership. The Senate, with its small size and consequent great opportunities for each member to make an effective bid for influence, produces many leaders of national stature. Its peculiar rules and customs may sometimes thwart the popular will; but the fact that "Senatorial courtesy" makes of each Senator a little king in a certain area has the great advantage, as Arthur Krock once remarked, that "it makes it worth a man's while to be a United States Senator." And as Lyndon Johnson has demonstrated, like Robert A. Taft before him, the Senate retains ample scope for effective democratic leadership. In the House, the opportunities for leadership in matters of national policy are notoriously limited, although an effective committee chairman may have considerable impact both within the chamber and in the country at large, especially in his dealings with the representatives of groups regularly appearing before his committee. In some measure the effectiveness of his leadership in his own constituency will be a function of the stature he attains in Congress.

As to our system of political parties, the implications of the general position I am taking have already been made apparent. Disciplined, programmatic national parties, even if they were attainable, would inflict upon the American political process a straitjacket entirely incompatible with the kind of leadership (flexible, permeating the whole social structure, and with the balance between leader and led never too one-sided) herein espoused. Once more, for the benefit of any who may be inclined to think the grass is greener elsewhere, the comment of a seasoned member of the House of Commons is apt. "We shall not progress," declares Sir Hartley Shawcross, "until Government and Opposition parties try to find out not how much they can exaggerate their differences and sabotage each other's efforts but how much they can make common cause."[30] But this is not to foreclose the question as to whether certain particular changes designed to achieve some increase in party discipline would be desirable.

X

Now what of the prevailing American temper? It is proper that we should keep a constant watch for changes in the popular mood and give thought to their significance. Yet we tread here on dangerous ground. Popular moods are elusive and often ephemeral. What is today's dangerous trend is likely to be tomorrow's almost-forgotten history. In such matters one must seek to steer a course between foolish complacency and frenetic alarmism. One recent writer proclaims, "what is happening today is that the mob, who were never a challenge when they were poor, who allowed the established monied classes to dominate their society while they were themselves struggling for economic independence, are now, under the stimulus of prosperity, developing the very tendencies that the Founding Fathers feared."[31] According to this interpretation, Senator Joseph R. McCarthy stood for, and brought to a temporary peak, a spirit that is still on the march and likely yet to do even more damage in the future than it has in the past. The keynotes of this mob spirit are mediocrity and anti-intellectualism. This is hardly a vision that bodes well for leadership; at least not for good leadership. But is there really any evidence, any ground for belief that this latest siege of "Know-Nothingness" is any more virulent than the bug that has always been lurking in the background in American society, subjecting us to uncomfortable attacks from time to time but with little indication of fatal potentialities? I have not seen it. On the contrary I am impressed by the way in which Sputnik seems to have touched off a wave of concern for providing special training for the exceptionally able—and not only for scientists, either.

David Riesman and Andrew Hacker and a host of others are greatly worried about conformism. Here again the fear is that those things that over a century ago men like Tocqueville and John Stuart Mill feared as consequences of democracy are finally catching up with us. Assuming for the moment that we are in fact losing our individualism, what is the significance of this development for political leadership? Only a few years ago a student of leadership listed "the decline of community" as one of the factors of modern times that threatened resolution of our problems by *submission* to leadership.[32] Now it is suggested that *too much* community pressure may enslave us. Of course both may be true. We may be swinging from one extreme to the other. But just as we avoided catastrophe in the first instance, so we may in the next. In any case we should examine the present situation a little more carefully in terms of its bearing on the topic in hand. Two quite different dangers are frequently cited. One is that, in a highly conformist society, there may be a dearth of leadership types. This is certainly possible. On the other hand, it must be noted that the demands upon leadership would be diminished by the very nature of a conformist society. There would be fewer divergent wills to be reconciled. The alternative threat is that such a society would fall prey to a dictator, or, more likely, that it would easily lend itself to manipulative domination.

This may indeed happen. It is possible that democratic man is becoming so sheep-like that he will willingly, perhaps gladly submit to some form of domination, whether of the dictatorial or of the subtle, manipulative type. I doubt very much that the swing of the pendulum will go that far or last that long. But this faith is little more than a hunch, with some foundation, I believe, in the past experience of such movements.

XI

It is especially fitting that the concluding remarks of a discussion that leaves so many questions unanswered should make some suggestions about areas for research.

It would be extremely helpful if a number of studies of leadership on particular policy problems and in policy areas were made. These could be directed toward studying the leadership process at all levels, and toward attempting to discover which of the various leadership tasks is being least adequately performed and why. Another valuable approach would be to seek to discover the impact of particular constitutional arrangements, such as length of tenure, size of constituency, and eligibility for reelection, on the quality of leadership. A great number of small comparative studies at the state as well as the national level should provide useful material for scientific generalization. A distinct but closely related series of studies might deal with the institutionalization of leadership in various contexts. For any given situation, for example, that of a Senator from a populous, industrialized state, what can staff aids accomplish? How well are these tasks being performed? What are the effects of institutionalizing his office upon him, upon his relations with other leaders and with his followers, and upon the type of person who tends to be selected for the job? Finally, still another type of study would be to examine the relations between particular leaders, both official and unofficial, and their followers. To what extent do they dominate? To what extent lead? To what extent are they led or influenced? And to what extent do they achieve real integration? What are their methods? Are their successes achieved by superior information, superior analysis, superior ability to relate their objectives with the values of their would-be followers, or some other element? Many of these questions could probably be answered, if at all, only by the development of new techniques of inquiry. Certainly the skills of the social psychologist would be called for.

It may not be out of order to suggest here, that *pari passu* with the development of understanding of the leadership phenomenon, we may strive for better training in the techniques of political leadership. Courses and even schools concentrating in this area, combining the impartation of scientific understanding with practical experience *via* the internship device and artificial experience by means of the case method, might contribute in two ways to the quality of American political leadership at nearly all levels. First, it might improve the work of men (and women) who would have been leaders in any event. Second, by adding respectability to the vocation of political leadership, it might add significantly to the number of able people who go into politics.

It is time to bring this discussion to a close. To summarize what has been said is clearly impracticable, and I hope unnecessary. It might be helpful, however, to relate my argument more systematically than has yet been done to the position of the other contributors, insofar as their contributions and mine meet.

Between Hartz and myself I believe there is a large measure of agreement. We concur in believing that classical democratic theory contained certain essential truths. For both of us the development of the individual is basic. He sees the state as coming back to protect the individual from the group. I would supplement this statement by arguing that the greater the opportunity for groups to share in policy-making, outside the formal structure of government, the greater is the incentive for group members to be active participants and for leadership within groups to be a two-way affair. Furthermore, I would stress that in this process, the line between elites and masses becomes less sharp, the middle ground becomes more thickly populated, and the relations between the various parts becomes increasingly reciprocal. In other words the masses not only control the elite, they supply it with ideas and with understanding as well.

With Lindblom, and especially with those parts of his discussion that most directly relate to my topic, I believe I am in essential agreement. Again, the supplementary element that I would like to add to his discussion of fragmented policy-making would be an emphasis upon what I have been calling the group-process.

It is between Beer and myself that the widest disagreements emerge. In large measure they are discussed above. To resolve our differences we would need answers to the following questions: (1) How does one measure "efficiency," and especially "coherence" of policy? (2) Does American policy-making meet these tests less well than British? (3) If so, could the disparity be corrected (by changed institutions) within our peculiar social (pluralistic) and ideological (atomistic) environment? (4) If the answer to the last two questions is in the affirmative, what would be the cost to democracy? (5) Finally, would it be worth the cost? Since to an important degree our differences revolve around the validity of Lindblom's concept of rational decision-making without overview, it is worth noting that much of what I have to say—for example, as to the role of leadership in making a pluralistic society sufficiently organic to work satisfactorily and as to the role of the institutionalization of leadership and the division of its functions—is applicable whether or not one accepts the thesis of rationality by fragmentation.

Finally, with Epstein as with Hartz and Lindblom, I would supplement rather than disagree. While admitting that foreign policy poses particularly serious problems for democratic leadership, I find grounds for long-run optimism in certain offsetting factors which arise in part out of the nature of democracy itself.

In addition to this cursory comparison of positions, it may

be worth while to select one or two major points for reiteration. I have argued that our commitment to democracy entails certain consequences with respect to the kind of leadership that will be typical, or at least toward which democracy will move insofar as it moves toward its ideal-type—bearing in mind that its tendency to move in this direction may be indefinitely held in check by other demands. Under conditions prevailing in industrialized societies it will tend toward a pluralistic and yet quasi-organic type of society, in which leadership is highly molecular or interstitial. It will be less spectacular than autocratic leadership and, at least in some circumstances, less quick to shift its direction. For all this it will be no less effective, at least with regard to domestic matters, but rather the contrary. The point is that, Mr. Fyfe and many others to the contrary notwithstanding,[33] democracy is *less* dependent than other forms of government upon the character and ability of *particular* leaders. There are several reasons for this fact, but perhaps the most important is that democracy's tasks are more widely dispersed.

Democracy and Foreign Policy

By Leon D. Epstein
University of Wisconsin

TRADITIONAL DEMOCRATIC POLITICAL theorists offered a simpler image of popular representative government than we can accept today. But even if they exaggerated the degree to which policy generally could be responsive to strictly individual rights and interests, they were able to treat foreign policy as an exception to the traditional image of popular control over decision-making. To take the classic example, John Locke's description of what he called the "federative power" contains the view that "what is to be done in reference to foreigners, depending much upon their actions and the variation of designs and interests, must be left in great part to the prudence of those who have this power committed to them, to be managed by the best of their skill for the advantage of the commonwealth."[1]

Locke, it is plain, thought of this unfettered executive control of foreign relations not only as a correct descriptive statement of fact, but also as an entirely proper arrangement. It was the way foreign policy was conducted and the way it ought to be conducted. His version of the classical image, in other words, corresponded with what he thought was the functioning reality. Or one might more reasonably say that he adjusted his image so that ordinary representative institutions did not extend to foreign policy-making, and that he did so because he could not see how, in the real world, foreign affairs could be made to fit the system he recommended for domestic affairs. Treating foreign policy in this way, as a special case, often appeared reasonable enough into the Nineteenth century. As universal manhood suffrage and mass democracy developed in the western world, their champions, though perhaps persisting in the

image of full popular control generally as Hartz has described it, could count foreign affairs as of marginal importance to newly enfranchised citizens, and so fit to be left
in the hands of the few.

However, especially in the United States and elsewhere
too on occasion, the image of popular control generally
seems not always to have been modified so as to make foreign policy an exception. Instead, attempts were made from
the start to subject all affairs to the pressures of the representative system, and so to have foreign policy-making conform to the general democratic image. But as Tocqueville
remarked in the 1830's, ignoring American international
difficulties in the first years of the Republic, the nation's
foreign policy consisted "more in abstaining than in acting."[2]
In his view the United States did not then face the full consequences of its constitutional arrangement and its democratic supposition which provided a measure of popular
control over policies of all sorts. Or, in Tocqueville's frame
of reference, American experience was not such as to test
adequately the hypothesis that a democratically governed
nation would conduct its foreign relations in a manner
inferior to that of nations governed by aristocrats.

The accepted image of Great Britain's foreign policy-
making process in the Nineteenth century conforms more
closely to the Lockean view. At least it has been widely
believed that even in the golden age of British parliamentary
institutions the conduct of international relations remained
removed from the ordinary pressures of representative government. Britain's considerable foreign policy business was
supposed to be, and presumably was thought to be in fact,
in the hands of a traditional governing class and, constitutionally, charged to the Crown. Yet the support of public
opinion, even though it was only a relatively narrow sector
of opinion that counted, was necessary to the successful
conduct of policy. Surely the Nineteenth century was a
period in which British foreign policy was the subject of
important parliamentary controversy, and the maintenance
of majorities in support of particular governments turned on
international as well as domestic issues. Accordingly, then,

parliamentary controversy on foreign affairs was extended to the country in the same way, limited though it was, as disagreement on home affairs.

Nevertheless the conduct of British foreign policy was conceived as the preserve of an elite, subject though it was to political criticism, and the claim for popular control, even if made, was not necessarily acknowledged when the suffrage was extended to the mass of the population. When Britain did enter the era of mass democracy, fairly late compared to the American experience, it was primarily for domestic matters, touching intimately and directly the lives of the masses of the population, that popularly elected parliaments were sought and subsequently employed. Despite continued public controversy over Britain's obviously important mid-Nineteenth century international concerns, the rising democracy did not have the same urgency about imposing its will in the foreign as in the domestic sphere. Neither the practice nor the image had to conform to the general democratic norm.

Before the end of the Nineteenth century, however, there were signs of change. The Eastern question and Imperial adventures engaged wide public attention, and in 1879–1880 there was a major effort by Gladstone, in his famous Midlothian speaking campaign, to place issues of foreign policy directly before the mass electorate. However, it is important that this was then considered a novelty, even though now it seems a forerunner of Twentieth century democratic practice. Then, in an era before modern mass military establishments, the cost in men and resources of failures in the conduct of foreign policy was not so painful as to make popular control an effective political rallying point. Furthermore, there was the optimistic Nineteenth century view, prevalent especially among liberal democrats, that an increasingly rational world would eliminate wars anyway. Some credence was lent this view by the long period without major conflicts which Britain enjoyed after the Napoleonic wars. Anything that tended to reduce the importance of foreign affairs in the lives of ordinary citizens made it easier to relegate the subject to specialists, in theory as well as in practice. The ideal was, no foreign policy beyond peaceful commercial transactions. Thus it was possible to avoid the question of reconciling the demands of foreign policy with the processes of popular control.

Much of socialist thought, in the late Nineteenth century and in the years before World War I, seems similarly to have avoided the problem. In extending egalitarianism from political to economic matters, democratic socialists often believed that foreign affairs would be settled or simplified by the establishment of a socialist order. Especially did this view prevail among those who accepted imperialism as exclusively the product of capitalist societies and so as something that, along with most of the rising foreign policy problems, could be eliminated entirely.

Generally it is fair to say that until World War I, despite some pressure from a fairly broad public to influence governments (at the time of the Boer War, for example), Britain along with most European nations, democratic and undemocratic, was free from serious attempts to institutionalize popular control of foreign policy. Undoubtedly, British statesmen were able to commit their nation without open consultation with the electorate or the electorate's representatives. Moreover, the democratic image, whatever its implications, was not regularly understood to require popular control in this area.

II

The first World War brought a change in attitudes toward foreign policy-making in democratic systems. The enormity of human and economic sacrifices demanded of the mass of the population, especially by conscription of manpower, meant that democrats found it hard to treat the subject-matter of foreign policy as something minor enough to be left to executive discretion. Such a gap in the democratic image of the state now seemed too large for ideological vitality to be maintained. Was the newly enfranchised population to have no authority in the one matter which, by this time, was so clearly and directly concerned with life and death—not just with frontier skirmishes by professional soldiers?

Thus the conception of a popularly-based governmental process came to be bluntly applied to foreign policy. The democratic image was now, contrary to Locke, understood to include foreign affairs on much the same footing as domestic; and efforts were made to have the functioning reality conform to the image. Government by the people, or at least government by representatives directly responsible and *responsive* to the people, became the program of much of the public newly concerned and aroused about international relations. The interwar years were the heyday of the belief in the virtues of popular control, and the belief was taken up by many intellectuals as well as by politicians. The movement was by no means purely demagogic. Some of its supporters were moved primarily by the plain desire to avoid war, which they thought the electorate was more likely to do than a largely independent governing authority, but they too believed that popular control of foreign policy was an article of the pure democratic faith. "Open covenants openly arrived at" was but one facet of the new democratic demand.

In Britain certain important institutional changes took place in the conduct of foreign policy despite the maintenance of a strong executive and the traditional diplomatic corps. Political leadership, often unschooled in international matters, intervened contrary to Foreign Office advice. Treaties and other matters of international import came to be debated much more frequently in Parliament. Furthermore popular sentiment was politically mobilized, especially for disarmament, for governmental abdication of its responsibilities to the League of Nations, and for various pacifist-minded programs—in short, for all the objectives which "informed opinion" in the 1930's, and especially afterwards, regarded as incompatible with interests and security of the British nation. Significantly, it was particularly the Labour party, the custodian of what Beer has called Radical democracy as well as the principles of a "socialist" foreign policy, which often took the leadership in fostering these objectives. Most broadly conceived, and epitomizing the assertion of popular opinion, was the Peace Ballot of 1935, in which eleven million Britons subscribed to the contradictory principles of disarmament and resistance to aggression by collective security.[3] Apparently less important, at least temporarily in Britain, was the older nationalist jingoism, which amounted to another form of mass pressure on the making of foreign policy.

Application of democratic principles to the conduct of American foreign policy in the interwar years took a different turn from that of Europe. Although there was a similar upsurge of demand for popular control, many democratic ideologists in the United States thought it feasible, with its more favorable geographical circumstances, to have the nation contract out of great-power affairs almost altogether, and thus return to the idyllic order of the Nineteenth century in which the United States needed no alliances and no international organizations to ensure its own security. It is now fashionable to dismiss this interwar isolationism as either wicked or mad. But the original impulse, as opposed to later demands of the interwar period for no foreign entanglements, deserves consideration as an honest, though futile, attempt of democrats to reconcile the requirements of conducting international relations with a simplistic democratic image. What was wanted was the reduction of those relations to simple and limited purposes which would not require, for their accomplishment, any great unrestrained power in the hands of the executive leadership of the nation. Pacifists thought this was possible without armaments at all, and the preparedness wing of isolationists, with some exceptions, believed that only a very modest military establishment was needed. Thus, assuming the absence of danger, the isolationists could consistently deny the need for executive discretion, outside legislative and popular competence, in important foreign affairs. There were just not supposed to be any important affairs of this sort, and so democracy could function, as was intended, in domestic matters, without having to be compromised by the absence of popular control of foreign policy.

The democratic instinct at the root of this advocacy is plainest in the earlier, or progressive and populist, stage of interwar isolationism. Then the principal isolationists were, and had been, also the most radical of democrats in their demands for popular control of the machinery of government generally. The senior La Follette was the most notable figure, but there were others in the same predominantly rural progressive tradition. And their support was only partly ethnic. The progressive image was that government ought to be as close to the people as possible; therefore, the practices they urged included open primaries, referenda, direct legislative responsiveness to the electorate, and public access to government records. If an active foreign policy in close concord with other nations demanded secrecy and executive discretion, then there was something wrong with such a foreign policy and it should not be maintained. The notion that the people could judge more appropriately than anyone else what was in their own interests was as fully accepted for international as for domestic affairs.

The climactic demand of primitive democracy, at the national level, was for the Ludlow Resolution. In this resolution, presented to the House of Representatives in 1935, a constitutional amendment was proposed which would require a national referendum to confirm a congressional declaration of war (except in event of invasion). Representative Ludlow's proposal was finally disposed of in 1937 by the narrow margin of 209 to 188, and only after presidential pressure for such disposition. Less far-reaching but with the same general intent of preventing, by prior legislation, governmental commitments in foreign affairs, was the measure actually enacted in the 1930's to keep the United States neutral through a prohibition on the sale of arms to belligerent nations. Some of these efforts imply, of course, an excessively legalistic faith as well as purist democratic doctrine. The same may be said for the residual isolationism represented by the more recently proposed Bricker Amendment which would, constitutionally, have limited discretion, and even the discretion of the national government as such, in the field of foreign affairs.

Manifest failure has been the result of all attempts to contract out of international power relations as a way of preserving the pristine image of democratic government from the qualifications realistically required for the conduct of an active and important foreign policy. Nor has the alternative, and sometimes complementary, attempt to establish popular control of foreign policy appeared successful. Here, however, a kind of success, but a most unwelcome one, is conceded to the advocates of popular control by their strongest critics. In particular, Walter Lippmann, who decidedly prefers the Lockean view that the ordinary processes of representative government are unsuited to the control of foreign policy, argues that the western democracies have in fact, and to their great disadvantage, subjected governmental leadership to popular control. Lippmann himself rejects what he regards as the false democratic image of the Twentieth century, but believes that it does unfortunately coincide with the functioning reality of foreign policy-making in the western world. He would have democratic nations alter their image of how policy-making should function, and accordingly change the actual process as well. In brief, Lippmann argues that the efficacy of foreign policy suffers from popular control or popular pressure since "the pressure of the electorate is normally for the soft side of the equations."[4]

Whether or not one accepts as factually correct Lippmann's description of the way foreign policy is actually made, it is usual to agree with him that policy ought not be subject to the pressures which he, along with advocates of popular control, assumes to be part of the pristine democratic image. To most students, that image seems as inappropriate to foreign policy-making as it seemed to Locke, and all the more so now that the limitations with respect to popular participation even in domestic policy-making are also so much taken for granted.

III

With the rejection of anything like the pure doctrine of popular control, those who might be considered the custodians of the democratic image have tried to work out a picture of the democratic process in which a very large element of executive discretion in the conduct of foreign affairs could be made to fit. Simply treating foreign affairs as an exception, more or less in the manner of Locke, has not been good enough for an age in which international relations have to be regarded almost permanently as the most important concern of the western democracies. The admission that foreign policy ought, more fully than domestic policy, to be in the hands of public officials heavily insulated from popular pressures calls for a refined image or model of democracy. Opinions of the mass electorate are somehow to be understood as playing a part in the political process; but without suggesting the same degree, limited though it may be, of popular decision-making tolerated for domestic affairs. Some role for the public in the foreign policy-making process, it is hoped, can be justified if democracy is to be substantially distinguished from dictatorship.

An orthodox contemporary answer to this problem is that of A. D. Lindsay. In his effort to revise the classical image of democratic government, the public should always be consulted. But the basis for doing so in foreign affairs is different from that in domestic matters. Whereas in domestic concerns, no matter how technical the subject, he believes that people generally are rightfully consulted because their own experience tells them "where the shoe pinches," he argues that this principle does not hold in foreign affairs because the subjects concerned are remote from ordinary experience. But nevertheless the public must be consulted in foreign affairs so that the government knows what or how much the people are prepared to do.[5] In other words, in order to have an effective foreign policy, those charged with making it must be assured that they are, or will be, supported. This highly instrumental way of dealing with the question may appear also to justify a governmental policy of manipulating or manufacturing the popular support being sought. Lindsay, however, assuredly wants to avoid just this result, and he specifically proposes popular consultation as an alternative to a dictatorship so controlling the public mind that it need not consult. At least Lindsay does not want to open the way to manipulation of consent.

How closely does Lindsay's conception of foreign policy-making conform to contemporary descriptions of the working reality? There are obvious difficulties. Plainly some policies have to be made by officials without waiting to learn what the public is prepared to support,[6] or even without having the means to learn except in the loosest intuitive sense. This holds for extremely large matters, such as American intervention in Korea in 1950, as well as for those ordinarily conceived as "merely administrative." Therefore, the customary way of explaining the role assigned to the public in actual fact is to say that mass opinion determines the "basic direction," the broad limits, or the "bounds to the area of maneuver available to those charged with responsibility."[7] At any rate, these appear to be representative samples of the considerable volume of writing on the general subject by American specialists deeply concerned with the broad problem of postwar foreign policy. One writer, Henry M. Wriston (who incidentally, unlike Lippmann, is optimistic about the workings of executive initiative along with popular opinion), is fairly explicit in suggesting the types of questions which the public can, and ought to, be asked to decide: for example, whether the United States should go it alone and whether the nation should pay the bill for deterrent armaments.[8] Granting that these questions have not been presented bluntly to the American public, either in a referendum or in a clear-cut electoral choice between competing party programs, it is reasonable to say that an answer in the form of a rough popular consensus has properly been assumed. Nevertheless what such a sensible assumption involves is a heavily intuitive interpretation of the democratic process: sensing, that is, what the public is willing to support by way of a foreign policy.

One of the most intimate descriptions of this relation of a foreign policy-maker to the public is that of Kenneth Younger, writing of his experience as a British Labour government Minister of State in the Foreign Office. "When I first cast my mind back upon my own experience," he writes, "I was somewhat shocked to find that I could not immediately recollect any occasion when I or my superiors had been greatly affected by public opinion in reaching important decisions." But, he adds, this first impression was wrong in the sense that public opinion affects ministers subconsciously:

". . . the government tends to identify itself almost unconsciously with a vaguely sensed general will, and no clear formulation of the pressure of public opinion upon government policy ever occurs."[9] This is hardly the popular control desired by the pristine democrat, and it is indeed a very sophisticated interpretation of the relation of policy-maker to public desire. The broad limits of the "vaguely sensed general will" allow a latitude that is surely different in kind from that which democratic ideology tolerates in the case of domestic policy-makers, whose decisions are meant to be directly influenced by the perceived interests of the affected public. American political leaders in foreign affairs do not, it is true, usually describe their situation as quite so detached as Younger's from immediate public pressures. There is little doubt, however, that the desired position for the foreign policy-maker remains one in which he is circumscribed by no more than the most general notions of what the public is willing to support in the long run.

This is some distance, it must be stressed, not only from the primitive view that the public initiates policy, but also from the view that the public decides broad principles, as presented by political leaders, leaving the details and the administration to the executive. Rather the sophisticated democratic version appears, for example, to justify the executive in pursuing a policy which he knows the public has not adopted and would not then adopt if asked to do so, but which policy he believes is, in fact, in accord with the basic direction of the nation, and will, therefore, in the long run be able to enlist support. The classic example, of course, is President Franklin D. Roosevelt's policy in the few years before American entry into World War II. Various acts hostile to the potential enemy powers amounted to a policy which almost assumed an eventual American involvement in the war, although the necessity for such involvement had appeared to have been denied vigorously by President Roosevelt, and his opponent, in the 1940 election campaign.[10] Although sharing Roosevelt's rather than Charles A. Beard's, conception of the need for American participation in World War II, it is possible to accept the view that the executive leadership fostered a policy, and a tremendously important one, without a direct public mandate and with only the sense of the future willingness of the public to accept the consequences, when they became apparent, of the American position in the world. The necessary qualification is that certain important steps in the Administration's policy development, notably Lend-Lease, did require congressional approval.

Partly because most democratic intellectuals (unlike the purist Beard) did in fact approve of Roosevelt's undertakings in foreign policy as well as of the main trends of postwar internationalism, there have been continued attempts to refine the democratic model beyond Lindsay's statement, so that it more nearly fits the facts of this kind of foreign policy-making. One fact that weighed heavily in this reconsideration was the demonstrated lack of public knowledge and comprehension of foreign affairs. This was not novel, and ignorance had always had to be taken into account in justifying public participation in domestic affairs. But postwar sample surveys documented this ignorance of international problems in impressive, even appalling, fashion, and in particular made it clear that the bulk of the public cared less and understood considerably less about foreign affairs than about the domestic policies more intimately affecting personal interests.[11] By now no one seems prepared to disagree with Max Beloff's assertion: "In the case of foreign affairs, where the given elements in a situation consist largely of the attitudes and intentions of foreign communities, to expect a very high level of information on the part of the electorate is surely utopian."[12] The mass of the population is aptly described as responding to international issues not with policy reactions but only with fluctuations in mood at times of crises; and since some advance policy is required in foreign affairs the electorate as a whole can hardly be useful in fixing policy.[13] For the bulk of people who inevitably lack the opportunity to develop an adequate frame of reference for international events, the most that is expected is that the "right" stereotypes of thought will be accepted and that expectations of immediate results from international policies will not become excessive.

Having thus realistically discounted the possible contribution of the mass public, the most perceptive and ingenious of the postwar democratic revisionists, Gabriel Almond, has developed the concept of a much smaller "attentive public." This is conceived as a public before whom the various official and unofficial elites of the policy-making and opinion-forming level can present competing points of view. Here, to the interested and informed go-to-meeting minority, the open discussion of foreign policy alternatives, presumed essential in the democratic process, can take place. As Almond says, this is a quality, not a quantity, market.[14] It follows that educational efforts in international affairs should be directed to the various elites and their attentive public, and not wasted on the uninterested mass public.

This, it is fair to say, is often the strategy of the Foreign Policy Association, the Council on Foreign Relations, many university institutes in adult education, and some book publication in the international field. Much of the discussion before the attentive public, it can be granted, is not to present alternatives for even this sector of opinion to choose, but to sell a particular line already adopted by a policy-making elite. Nonetheless the need to obtain approval of the attentive public, if this need be acknowledged, is itself an important democratic element. This is to use the word "democratic" in a somewhat different sense from that associated with the earlier democratic image or the justification for universal suffrage. Although the views of the attentive public, once accepted, might filter down to sections of the mass public, this is hardly presented as crucial in this new model. The public that counts in Almond's conception is one whose numbers cause it to resemble, in its proportion of a given community, the section of the population enfranchised in mid-Nineteenth century Britain or the proportion whom Aristotle in his polity counted as citizens. The "people," in the earlier democratic sense, are passive elements with reference to policy-making even though they cast ballots—for the purpose, it appears, of assuring the policy-makers that the mass is prepared to support (in Lindsay's terms) the policies already adopted by the political elite and accepted by the attentive public. Thus the picture of the way foreign policy-making ought to work in a democratic society is adjusted to the way it is thought to work, or thought to be capable of working, in practice.

This may well be regarded also as an up-to-date democratic model or image for all policy-making, domestic as well as foreign. However, there remains one crucial difference, if not in the general conception, at least in the working models derived from it. In domestic policy-making, the attentive public presumably consists largely of individuals or groups with perceived interests at stake, and it is now usually conceived that domestic policy emerges as a result of compromise or adjustment of those interests. Moreover, as Hartz suggests, the anxieties we may have because this process departs from the classical democratic image, are largely fantastic. Accordingly, among both practitioners and intellectuals, this process of group politics is gradually gaining acceptance, even legitimacy. But in making foreign policy, the reconciliation of image and reality is not so easy. Insofar as the attentive public should happen to consist of groups with perceived interests, for example in tariffs or particular overseas investments, the determination of national policy according to these interests is not considered desirable in the same way. On the other hand, as appears true of many large foreign affairs issues, the attentive public may consist of citizens with few if any perceived direct interests. Then the question arises whether this public, whose knowledge is general and abstract, is competent in the same way as is the public for domestic issues.[15] For particulars it may be dependent on government sources, and therefore more open to manipulation, than would be true for the domestic attentive public. Even the most highly educated citizens are bound to find foreign policy questions far removed from their own experience and so more difficult to decide by the usual rational processes applied to questions of more intimate concern. This, of course, neglects the old-fashioned idea that disinterest and detachment make for "purer" public decisions in the national interest.

IV

The revised democratic image in which foreign policy is

presented by the executive to a special attentive, but largely passive, public is meant to be consistent with the achievement of what Beer has referred to as coherence in governmental policy. Coherent policy is always a prime desideratum in foreign affairs, and such models as there are of actual policy-making functions stress the need for adjustment of representative institutions in order to achieve coherence.

The term "coherence" is here considered as relating mainly to the political apparatus designed to produce effective policy. The assumption is that foreign policy must involve planning and continuity to be effective, and that the machinery of government should be adjusted to that end. This is not simply a matter of achieving policy consistency, since radical changes, planned surprises and even apparent inconsistencies may be effective weapons of policy. But these very results, it is assumed, require a unity in policy-making. Understandably, it is the American political system which has been most critically examined with respect to its capacity for coherence, since the United States has been thought to suffer generally on this count by comparison with Great Britain. Foreign affairs seem to present only a more acute problem than the achievement of coherence in the domestic sphere.

The difficulties are well illustrated by the effort to evolve contemporary models of foreign policy-making in terms of certain specific American institutional forms. Three in particular command notice: presidential- or executive-congressional relations, the competitive party system, and public discussion based on relatively free access to information. In all three instances, a need appears to bend the democratic tradition and practice to demands for coherence in foreign policy.

Working out the role of the legislative body is the most familiar problem, made especially sharp in the United States because the understood function of Congress, unlike that of the British Parliament, is to make policy and not simply debate it. At the very least, Congress is traditionally expected to share the policy-making role with the executive, and to do so to a large extent in foreign as well as domestic affairs. Certainly American legislators, claiming to represent popular opinion, customarily challenge the executive's conduct of foreign policy. That this has been so is a main particular of Walter

Lippmann's indictment of western democracies in the Twentieth century.[16] While Lippmann does not sharply distinguish between British and American experiences on this score, there seems little doubt that the United States provides the leading case. In the postwar years the congressional part in American foreign policy-making has taken on new dimensions, even as executive initiative, demanded by events, has also grown. This is the result of the increased scope and complexity of foreign affairs, particularly of the expansion of international programs requiring appropriations.[17] More of Congress's powers have become relevant to the conduct of foreign policy, and the tendency has been to exert these powers. Moreover, the committee and staff system in Congress provides a level of information which enables Congressmen to operate in a style virtually impossible for an ordinary backbench member of the House of Commons. On the surface, then, the threat of incoherence in executive-legislative conflict, if only through delay and uncertainty, would appear to have been magnified, and so most observers of the process conclude. The criticism of Congress becomes even more pointed when the legislative power is used, as it was by Senator Joseph R. McCarthy, to rally mass opinion against the official and unofficial policy elites.

"Interbranch friction," it has commonly been said, cannot be tolerated any longer in foreign affairs.[18] However, the stock political science remedy of constitutional reform to make American legislative-executive relations more nearly approximate the British cabinet system is now seldom taken seriously. Instead most of us have in mind a model of presidential-congressional collaboration, retaining the existing institutional framework but allowing the President a good deal of discretion in the actual conduct of policy.[19] Only the broad outlines of the policy would be the result of collaboration, and this presumably on presidential initiative. To a large extent, this model is derived from the way in which presidential-congressional relations have been thought actually to work in certain favorable circumstances. But there is hardly yet enough research to be certain that collaboration of this sort is, or even can be, a norm for behavior in the American system.[20]

The second institution which often seems to require adaptation to the purposes of a foreign policy-making model is the party system. The common suggestion here is the same one that is advocated as the means to achieve greater coherence in domestic policy. Each major party is supposed to become more responsible for, and more united on, a program, and so supply the coherence. Included, of course, is the idea that a party which happened to control both branches of government could achieve presidential-congressional collaboration through its own internal coherence. However, there is doubt about the applicability of this responsible party model to foreign policy, and in fact grave doubt in this regard about the appropriateness of the whole notion of the modern political scientist that highly integrated competitive parties constitute the health of the democratic state. Two responsible parties each with a coherent but different program are less attractive possibilties in foreign than in domestic affairs. Their respective programs would presumably be meant to appeal to the electorate broadly considered, including that part of it which is inattentive to foreign policy issues. Unless the differences in foreign policy presented to the electorate were fraudulent, it is hard to see how this model derived from domestic concerns could operate effectively in an area in which substantive policy is not supposed to be decided by the shifting verdicts of popular elections. Instead of arguing that parties should become more clearly programmatic with respect to foreign policy, it may be contended that they should become less so. Coherence in party structure, with each party coherent about a different policy, looks incompatible with the coherence usually sought for government itself in the conduct of foreign affairs.

Whether parties do in fact provide foci for different foreign policy commitments is an important researchable question. There is some suggestion even in the United States that party identification and particular international attitudes are associated, and that party may mold foreign policy attitudes, at least at certain crucial times.[21] Evidently British political parties, the models of coherence on domestic policy, can also serve as agencies for sharply differentiated foreign policies. A leading recent case is provided by the Suez crisis of 1956, when, with but a few exceptions, the Labour party took a view radically opposed to the Conservative government's decision to intervene by force in Egypt. So sharp a foreign policy difference between the parties is probably exceptional, but the Suez case does show how a high degree of general coherence of each political party may be transferred almost intact from the domestic arena. The consequences deserve careful critical study.

Seldom, however, does the divergence of parties on foreign policy appear so meaningful as it did in Britain during the Suez crisis. Broadly speaking, nations are not usually willing or able to shift their international commitments in the way that such divergence implies. Thus party followers, if devoted to what they regard as the special foreign policy of their party, are readily disappointed when their leaders move from opposition to office. As a British ambassador to the United States has said, "a political party has far less choice in its international than in its domestic politics, and far less control over events."[22] This was the lesson of experience after World War II for the British Labour party when its zealous rank-and-file, after years of juxtaposing their "socialist foreign policy" to that of the Conservatives, found their party leadership, while in office, embracing the doctrine of "continuity" in international relations. Similarly, if not so poignantly, American Republicans suffered disillusionment when they realized that their party's return to power in 1953 did not substitute either liberation or noninvolvement for the containment policy they had opposed. In light of such frustrations, it is reasonable, and it happens in Britain, that party leaders urge their followers not to commit the party, in advance of taking office, to any set international program.

In short, it seems hard to fit the competitive party system, especially in its more highly developed forms, into any acceptable model of foreign policy-making. It is no wonder that discussion of international issues is often urged as properly non-partisan, bi-partisan, or even extrapartisan.[23] The most that can be left for party competition in a model for achieving coherent foreign policy-making is a certain amount of debate at the margins; for example, on improving administrative practices or on providing slightly less foreign aid. These questions involve no more than incremental changes, to utilize Lindblom's language, and so are consistent with fairly long-term government planning. Furthermore, this view of the nature of party competition may correspond to the working reality of modern democratic government in domestic as well as foreign affairs. It is possible that parties themselves, along with the advocates of policy-oriented responsible parties, exaggerate the differences in their respective positions generally. Even if such exaggeration is inevitably a part of electoral competition, in which an opposition party in particular must dramatize the changes it promises, it need hardly follow that substantial changes can or actually do take place. The price for continuity, as has already been suggested, need only be frustration for party zealots, and they are likely to be a distinct minority on foreign as on domestic questions.

The third and more general institutional feature, public discussion based on relatively free access to information, is probably the most troublesome of all in relation to the model required for coherent foreign policy. And it is crucial to much of what has been said about the working of other democratic political institutions. The degree to which information vital to an understanding of foreign affairs is publicly available obviously determines the usefulness of the roles available to the legislative branch and to political parties. Yet it is widely assumed that some significant information, certainly that relating to military capabilities, is necessarily secret. How much and how vital this secret information may be remains unknown except to those who make the decisions as to what should be secret. Thus this factor is hard to evaluate, though the overwhelming importance of missile-capability data, necessarily withheld in detail, provides some idea of what is missing from public discussion. Obviously, however, the process of rational discussion of policy encompassed in Hartz's classical image of democracy is rendered increasingly unworkable to the degree that access to information is restricted.

Another equally troubling aspect of the need to hold back information in order to achieve an effective foreign policy arises in the propaganda field. Here the occasional usefulness of deliberately misleading antagonistic foreign powers can conflict with the tradition of supplying accurate explanations of governmental policy to the domestic public. In other words, a model for the effective conduct of foreign policy indicates propaganda lines incompatible with the supply of truthful information for public discussion of governmental policy, and, with reference to the democratic image, the spectre of manipulation emerges again. Usually it is thought that the United States at least falls short of the model in this respect; that is, the American government sacrifices propaganda advantages when and if these conflict with the demands of straightforward domestic discussion. Secretary of State Dulles said as much in April, 1958 when he told his journalistic inquisitors, at the time of an evident Russian propaganda victory in announcing the suspension of nuclear tests: "We operate, as is visible right here, in terms of a free and independent and highly intelligent press. If I came before you with something that was phony you would recognize it in a minute and tear it apart publicly."[24] This, he explained, made inevitably for American disadvantages in the propaganda field.

Moreover, it can just as well be added, living up to the dictates of the democratic process limits a government in a wider field than simply propaganda. The demand for a prior supply of public information about prospective governmental policy would, if met, restrict generally the opportunity for sharp changes in diplomatic strategy.[25]

V

From the effort to relate democratic institutions to a working model of coherent foreign policy-making, there emerges a specification of some of the difficulties earlier observed to have been implicit in the development of a revised and sophisticated image of democracy. Notably the scope demanded in foreign policy for executive authority is so great, and accordingly the role for institutional expression of public opinion so limited and passive, that the question arises whether even the revised democratic image of policy discussion before an attentive public can or does correspond to these demands of effective policy-making.

That image, to have vitality at all, would have to allow at

least a significant portion of the population a measure of choice in deciding to support governmental policy. But for the very reason that this public support is so manifestly essential if policy is to be effective, it seems doubtful that a meaningful choice between support and non-support can be exercised by the attentive public, or any public. Governmental leaders may have an overwhelming need to secure agreement on a policy already formulated and probably in effect more or less continuously.

The case for what looks like manipulation of opinion by government leaders tends to be strengthened by the absence, on foreign policy issues, of the kind of perceived interests which citizens are thought to possess with respect to domestic issues touching their own lives. Then too the nature of foreign policy seems to require that certain information be kept from the public in the name of military secrecy, or even of proposed surprise in the propaganda or diplomatic fields.

So understood, coherence in foreign policy-making appears to require a functioning political model in which the elected executive authority is entrusted with the formulation of policy, much as Walter Lippmann believes necessary. The only effective limits on this authority are then no more than those imposed by the very broadest strategic goals which a nation has in common and on which it is not consulted in any formal institutional way. That the public, attentive or otherwise, should be prepared to support governmental policy thus becomes but another task for government's leaders to accomplish.

The question whether such a model conforms more closely to the reality of recent policy-making than does the popular pressure model which Lippmann deplores might at least partially be answered by research. From what we know now concerning the United States and Great Britain, it appears possible that the functioning political reality reflects a good deal less internal coherence than the "ideally effective" foreign policy-making model suggests, although hardly approximating the image of effective popular control.

A particularly manageable research question is how much, and in what ways, the executive's conduct of foreign policy is affected by such debate as is carried on before the attentive public. That there is such a debate is obvious enough, from British as well as American experience during the Cold War. Furthermore much of the debate is carried on by critics of governmental policy who, even if outside of the executive apparatus, can be well-informed. Some of the critics derive their information from previous experience in the conduct of foreign policy, before their party was converted from office-holding to opposition. Others, of whom members of American congressional foreign affairs committees are preeminent, retain access to detailed knowledge even when their party does not control the executive branch. Still others, like Walter Lippmann himself, are non-governmental specialists of recognized stature. Then there are academic institutes as well. These critics at least, if not their attentive public, do rival the executive authority's informational scope, even to the extent of maintaining international sources through personal and political acquaintance overseas. Accordingly, they may be much less subject to manipulation than the bulk of the public, and perhaps therefore able to impose a check on the degree to which opinion generally could be manipulated. To be sure, this would not be a "popular" check.

Research along this line would not, it is well understood, provide the answer to the question of what model of foreign policy-making ought to be adopted as a standard by which to measure a democratic government's performance. But it would lead to some knowledge of what model most nearly corresponds to the reality of experience. Furthermore, we might well learn how much to be concerned about the evident need to yield even the remnants of the popular control image to the needs of coherent foreign policy-making. If it were found that informed non-governmental elite critics played significant roles, there would be some solace for the democratic ideologist.

Notes

DEMOCRACY: IMAGE AND REALITY
By Louis Hartz

1. For a general discussion of the reaction against the Enlightenment, see the brilliant book by Judith N. Shklar, *After Utopia: The Decline of Political Faith* (Princeton, 1957).

2. John Taylor, *A Definition of Parties, or the Political Effect of the Paper System Considered* (Philadelphia, 1794).

NEW STRUCTURES OF DEMOCRACY: BRITAIN AND AMERICA
By Samuel H. Beer

1. T. C. Wyller, *Nyordning og Motstand,* with an English summary (Oslo, 1958), 315.

2. See E. S. Mason, "The Apologetics of 'Managerialism,'" *Journal of Business of the University of Chicago,* XXXI (January, 1958), 1-11.

3. See S. H. Beer, "The Representation of Interests in British Government: Historical Background," *American Political Science Review,* LI (September, 1957), 613-650, especially at 614-628.

4. *Ibid.,* 628-645.

5. *Ibid.,* 645-650.

6. See A. H. Birch, *Small Town Politics: A Study of Political Life in Glossop* (London, 1959), 85-94, and references given there.

7. See S. E. Finer, *Anonymous Empire: A Study of the Lobby in Great Britain* (London, 1958), and J. D. Stewart, *British Pressure Groups, Their Role in Relation to the House of Commons* (Oxford, 1958).

8. Mason, *op. cit.,* and references given there.

9. Lowell counted as a party vote a division in which at least 90 per cent of one party voted in favor and at least 90 per cent of the other party voted against. A. L. Lowell, "The Influence of Party upon Legislation in England and America," *Annual Report of the American Historical Association for 1901* (Washington, 1902), 319-542.

10. R. T. McKenzie, *British Political Parties* (New York, 1955).

11. *Ibid.,* 587.

12. Sir Ivor Jennings, *Parliament* (Cambridge, England, 1948), Chapter V, "The Art of Management."

13. Chester I. Barnard, *The Functions of the Executive* (Cambridge, Massachusetts, 1938).

14. W. L. Guttsman, "Aristocracy and the Middle Class in the British Political Elite 1886-1916," *British Journal of Sociology*, V (1954).

15. Mason, *op. cit.*, 3.

16. S. E. Finer, *op. cit.*, 3.

17. Since this was written, the Campaign for Nuclear Disarmament, a promotional group with much of the old Radical flavor, has risen to prominence, exerting substantial influence at least on the policy of the Labour Party.

18. The Transport and General Workers' Union, the National Union of General and Municipal Workers, the Amalgamated Engineering Union—which among them include 30 per cent of all unionists affiliated to the TUC.

19. Hugh A. Clegg, "Strikes," *Political Quarterly*, XXVII (January-March, 1956), 31-35.

20. John A. Mack, "Trade Union Leadership," in *Ibid.*, 77.

21. Data on British associations are from P.E.P., *Industrial Trade Associations: Activities and Organization* (London, 1957).

22. S. E. Finer, "The Federation of British Industries," *Political Studies*, IV (February, 1956), 62.

23. R. W. Gable, "N.A.M.: Influential Lobby or Kiss of Death?", *Journal of Politics*, 15 (May, 1953), 257. See also A. S. Cleveland, "N.A.M.: Spokesman for Industry?", *Harvard Business Review*, 26 (1948), 353-371.

24. William J. Fellner, *Competition among the Few: Oligopoly and Similar Market Structures* (New York, 1949). See also Thomas C. Schelling, "An Essay on Bargaining," *American Economic Review*, 45 (June, 1956), at 218-283.

25. Avery Leiserson, *Administrative Regulation: A Study in Representation of Interests* (Chicago, 1942), 162.

26. E. Pendleton Herring, *Public Administration and the Public Interest* (New York, 1936), 192.

27. For a brief sketch see *Consultation with Industry: A History of the Office of Industry Advisory Committees of the N.P.A.* (Washington, United States Department of Commerce, 1953). This is Report Number 19 of Historical Reports on Defense Production. See also *Advisory Committees,* (Part I-V), subcommittee of the House Committee on Government Operations, 84 Congress, 2 Session (1956); Hearings before the same subcommittee on H.R. 3378, 85 Congress, 1 Session (1957); H.R. Report 576 on H.R. 7390, 85 Congress, 1 Session (1957).

28. Donald C. Blaisdell, *Economic Power and Political Pressures*, Monograph 26, TNEC, Investigation of Concentration of Economic Power, 76 Congress, 3 Session (Washington, 1941), at 57 and 70.

29. Henry A. Turner, "How Pressure Groups Operate," *Annals of the American Academy of Political and Social Sciences*, 319 (September, 1958), at 66 and *passim*.

30. Hugh A. Bone, "Political Parties and Pressure Group Politics," in *Ibid.*, at 79. Bone summarizes the findings of the *Final Report of the Special Committee to Investigate Political Activities, Lobbying and Campaign Contributions*, United States Senate, 85 Congress, 1 Session (May, 1957).

31. S. E. Finer, *Anonymous Empire*, 67-8.

32. J. H. Millett, "British Interest Group Tactics: A Case Study," *Political Science Quarterly* (March, 1957).

33. Turner, *op. cit.*, 68.

34. Nigel Nicolson, *People and Parliament* (London, 1958), at 50 and 170.

35. E. E. Schattschneider, "United States: The Functional Approach to Party Government," in Sigmund Neumann, Ed., *Modern Political Parties: Approaches to Comparative Politics* (Chicago, 1956), 194-215.

36. Max Weber's discussion of "rationality" as a quality of action by an individual or a collectivity is relevant to this criterion. See Weber, *The Theory of Social and Economic Organization*, Translated by A. M. Henderson and Talcott Parsons (New York, 1947). References to the discussion by Weber and Parsons are given in the index.

37. Stephen K. Bailey, *The Condition of Our National Political Parties*, A Fund for the Republic Pamphlet (New York, 1959). See for references to the controversy over party government.

38. Herring, *op. cit.*, 377.

DEMOCRACY AND ECONOMIC STRUCTURE
By CHARLES E. LINDBLOM

1. James Burnham, *The Managerial Revolution* (New York, 1941); C. Wright Mills, *The Power Elite* (New York, 1956).

2. Clark Kerr, "Wage Relationships—the Comparative Impact of Market and Power Forces," Reprint of Institute of Industrial Relations, University of California at Berkeley, Reprinted from John T. Dunlop, Ed., *The Theory of Wage Determination* (New York, 1957).

3. E. Pendleton Herring, *The Politics of Democracy* (New York, 1940).

4. Joseph Goldstein, *The Government of British Trade Unions* (Glencoe, Illinois, 1952).

5. Seymour M. Lipset, Martin A. Trow, and James S. Coleman, *Union Democracy* (Glencoe, Illinois, 1956).

6. Clinton S. Golden and Harold J. Ruttenberg, *The Dynamics of Industrial Democracy* (New York, 1942).

7. Burnham, *op. cit.*; and Mills, *op. cit.*

8. Talcott Parsons, "The Distribution of Power in American Society," *World Politics*, X (October, 1957), 123-143; and Charles E. Lindblom, "In Praise of Political Science," *World Politics*, IX (January, 1957), 240-253.

9. Arnold A. Rogow, *The Labour Government and British Industry 1945-1951* (Ithaca, New York, 1955).

10. For suggestions, see C. Addison Hickman and Manford H. Kuhn, *Individuals, Groups, and Economic Behavior* (New York, 1956), Chapters 2 and 3.

11. For example, Luther Gulick and Lyndall Urwick, Eds., *Papers on the Science of Administration* (New York, 1937); E. Pendleton Herring, *Public Administration and the Public Interest* (New York, 1936); Dwight Waldo, *The Administrative State* (New York, 1948); John D. Kingsley, *Representative Bureaucracy* (Yellow Springs, Ohio, 1944); and others.

12. For example, Robert A. Dahl, *A Preface to Democratic Theory* (Chicago, 1956); E. Pendleton Herring, *The Politics of Democracy, op. cit.*; Earl Latham, *The Group Basis of Politics* (Ithaca, New York, 1952); E. E. Schattschneider, *Party Government* (New York, 1942); and David B. Truman, *The Governmental Process* (New York, 1951).

13. For discussion of possibilities, see Henry A. Landsberger, *Hawthorne Revisited* (Ithaca, New York, 1958); and Harold L. Wilensky, "Human Relations in the Work-place: An Appraisal of Some Recent Research," in C. M. Arensberg, *et al.*, Eds., *Research in Industrial Human Relations* (New York, 1957).

14. Bertrand de Jouvenel, *The Ethics of Redistribution* (Cambridge, England, 1951), 67.

15. William H. Whyte, *The Organization Man* (New York, 1956).

16. Rogow, *op. cit.*

17. Bernard R. Berelson, Paul F. Lazarsfeld, and William N. McPhee, *Voting* (Chicago, 1954).

18. Charles E. Lindblom, *Bargaining: The Hidden Hand in Government* (Santa Monica, California, 1955); and Lindblom, *Decision-Making in Taxation and Expenditure* (Mimeograph, New York, 1959).

19. Lindblom, *Bargaining,* and Lindblom, *Decision-Making.*

20. Adolph Sturmthal, *The Tragedy of European Labour 1918-1939* (New York, 1943).

21. James Tobin, "The Eisenhower Economy and National Security: Two Views, Dollars, Defense, and Doctrines," *The Yale Review,* XLVII (1958), 321-334.

DEMOCRACY AND LEADERSHIP
By J. Roland Pennock

1. Hamilton Fyfe, *The Nineteenth Century and After,* 129 (1941), 465-484, 465.

2. It cannot be stressed too much that I am dealing here with "pure types," such as never appear in real life. In practice the distinction between leadership and domination is of course a matter of degree. Many functions of leadership are performed by

the dominator; most leaders rely in some measure upon domination. These facts do not detract from the importance of the distinction. Many, if not most important distinctions turn in practice on matters of degree. Compare the distinction between Aristotle's "good" and "perverted" forms of government.

The definition of leadership here adopted departs from that advocated by Lasswell and Kaplan by including those whose influence (power) is not "formalized by the perspectives of authority" (Harold D. Lasswell and Abraham Kaplan, *Power and Society: A Framework for Political Inquiry* [New Haven, 1950], 152F). For the purposes of the present discussion the broader definition appears to be preferable because it is leadership in this sense, not simply in the sense of "legitimate power," that critics like Fyfe and many others declare democracy lacks.

It should be noted that leadership as here defined does not disregard the fact that, in a continuing relationship of leading and following, the leader is given the benefit of the doubt by his followers and has less need to exercise the arts of persuasion than he did at the outset. Where we draw the line between willing followership and coerced or automatic response to domination or manipulation is never an easy task to determine. This fact is what makes the vision of *Walden Two* so fearful; we might be there without knowing it!

For this discussion, I have drawn heavily upon the following sources: *Encyclopedia of the Social Sciences*, "Leadership" (Richard Schmidt); Alvin W. Gouldner, Ed., *Studies in Leadership* (New York, 1950), especially 17-18; Paul Pigors, *Leadership or Domination* (Cambridge, Massachusetts, 1935), Part I.

3. I speak of "primary" political power, as institutionalized in the vote, to exclude the additional power a person may secure through election to office, gaining influence over others, or otherwise.

4. Lasswell and Kaplan, *op. cit.*, 227.

5. *Cf.* Anthony Downs' demonstration that, in his model democracy, in the absence of uncertainty arising out of lack of information, there would be no need for leadership. Anthony Downs, *An Economic Theory of Democracy* (New York, 1957), 87. It should be noted, however, that Downs is speaking only of a limited kind of leadership and does not postulate conditions that would eliminate the necessity for all leadership as here defined.

6. See Francis E. Lowe and Thomas C. McCormick, "A Study of the Influence of Formal and Informal Leaders in an Election Campaign," *Public Opinion Quarterly*, 20 (1957), 651-662. This study indicates that opinion leaders tend to have least influence among the politically alert.

It will be observed that for simplicity's sake, I have violated strict logic by including anarchy or "voluntarism" as a form of government, which it technically is not. In the discussion above, however, I have spoken of that most extreme form of democracy that most nearly approaches the anarchic limit that it cannot reach without ceasing to be government.

7. "Authoritarian and Democratic Leadership," in Gouldner, Ed., *op. cit.* (Note 2), 396. Bagehot's famous distinction between the "ceremonial" and the "efficient" functions of government has strongly elitist overtones.

8. Walter Lippmann, *The Public Philosophy* (Boston, 1955), 30.

9. John Plamenatz, "Electoral Studies and Democratic Theory, I: A British View," *Political Studies*, 6 (January, 1958), 1. As a matter of fact Plamenatz's own view as set forth in this article ascribes a more understanding and perhaps more active, though not more articulate role to the voter than is fully in keeping with autocratic democratic theory.

10. Ideal-types seldom find pure expression in the writings of any given individual. Doubtless Bentham and James Mill envisaged some role for leadership and perhaps the same may be said for the vaguely defined "classical image" of democracy. I speak here of a *tendency* that is, I believe, easily discernible in these theories. *Insofar* as this tendency prevails, we might think of radical democracy as occupying a position somewhere toward the "voluntarist" end of the diagram, while elitist democracy would be to the right of center.

11. *Cf.* Hans Kelsen, "Foundations of Democracy," *Ethics*, 66 (1955), 32.

12. The theory of group-equilibrium is less easy to identify with a particular writer than are those previously discussed. Writers like David Easton, who discuss its value for analytical purposes, do not use it as a model of how democracy ought to operate. But, in the works of many political scientists from Bentley to Truman, there are at least strong overtones of suggestion that pressure-group politics, properly channeled by institutional devices, works in much the same beneficent fashion ascribed by radical democrats to the politics of individual self-interest.

13. The names of A. D. Lindsay and Mary P. Follett properly come first to mind in this connection.

14. Kelsen, *loc. cit.*, 32; T. D. Weldon, *States and Morals* (London, 1946), especially 186-190.

15. See Pigors, *op. cit.* (Note 2), 3-6.

16. See Elmer Cornwell, "Coolidge and Presidential Leadership," *Public Opinion Quarterly*, 21 (1957), 265-278. To some it may seem somewhat paradoxical to extend the concept of leadership this far. Nothing in the argument of this chapter depends on doing so. Bertrand de Jouvenel uses the term "authority" for something close to what I have called "leadership," and then applies the term *"dux,"* or "leader" to one who exercises authority intermittently and actively, while the *"rex,"* or rectifier is more passive though more constant in his exercise of authority by such

means as laying down rules of conduct, enforcing contracts, and arbitrating disputes. Bertrand de Jouvenel, *Sovereignty, an Inquiry into the Political Good,* Translated by J. F. Huntington (Cambridge, England, 1957), Chapter 2, especially 34.

17. Harry M. Scoble, "Yankeetown: Leadership in Three Decision-Making Processes" (Mimeograph, Paper presented at meetings of the American Political Science Association, September 6-8, 1956).

18. Richard Neustadt, "The Presidency at Mid-Century," *Law and Contemporary Problems,* 21 (1956), 609-645.

19. Cornwell, *loc. cit.,* 278.

20. John Locke, *Second Treatise of Civil Government,* Paragraph 96.

21. Jean Jacques Rousseau, *The Social Contract,* Translated by G. D. H. Cole (London, 1915), Book IV, Chapter 2.

22. It is worth remarking that one is not reduced to a choice between centralized decision-making with complete overview and the opposite extreme of wholly fragmented decision-making with no overview. More usual and doubtless for many purposes more desirable decision-making techniques involve partial fragmentation and imperfect overview. Members of a Congressional committee, for instance, may act on a bill having an important bearing on inflation with *some* knowledge of economists' recommendations (assuming essential agreement among economists!) and partly out of consideration of this information while also being governed in part by consideration of particular interests of their own constituents or out of considerations of partisan advantage.

23. Downs, *op. cit.* (Note 5), Chapter 4.

24. It is of course possible that under certain circumstances (those prevailing in this country today, for instance) a high degree of approximation to the democratic ideal as here defined is undesirable. If in fact such dispersed leadership fails to produce that amount of agreement and positive, wise action that our problems require, and if it appears that the situation in this respect would be bettered if we adopted institutions that provided for more "big" leadership and for leaders who leaned further in the direction of domination, we would be foolish not to modify our institutions accordingly. It is my personal conviction that there is no present need to abandon or substantially modify our pluralistic system. Here of course I may be wrong. Moreover, one must recognize that it is not a question of either-or, except as a matter of degree and emphasis. One need not adopt the ideal of disciplined national political parties, for instance, to believe that certain steps that would tend to minimize the present weakness of American parties might be desirable.

Little if anything has been said in our discussions about France. It seems probable that the institutions of the Fourth Republic made too little allowance for a counterweight to pluralism. (See the remarks in the next section.) Whether the constitution of the Fifth Republic has struck a better balance or gone to the other extreme is a matter for debate, and experience.

25. Max Lerner, *America as a Civilization* (New York, 1957), 374.

26. *Ibid.*, 376.

27. L. S. Amery, *Thoughts on the Constitution* (London, 1947), 86.

28. Lerner, *op. cit.*, 372.

29. Ruth C. Silva, "The Presidential Constituency and Party Alignment" (Mimeograph, Paper read at meetings of the American Political Science Association, September 6, 1957).

30. Quoted by Woodrow Wyatt in "Has the House of Commons Had Its Day?", *The New York Times Magazine* (April 13, 1958), 3.

31. P. Worsthorne, "America's Crisis of Prosperity," *The Twentieth Century*, 160 (1956), 387-396, 392.

32. Lester G. Seligman, "The Study of Political Leadership," *American Political Science Review*, XLIV (1950), 904-915, 906.

33. Fyfe, *loc. cit.* (Note 1), 465.

DEMOCRACY AND FOREIGN POLICY
By LEON D. EPSTEIN

1. John Locke, *Second Treatise of Civil Government*, Chapter XII, 147.

2. Alexis de Tocqueville, *Democracy in America*, I (New York, 1945), Edition of Henry Reeves text edited by Phillips Bradley, 234.

3. Winston S. Churchill, *The Second World War*, Volume I, *The Gathering Storm* (Boston, 1948), 169-70.

4. Walter Lippmann, *The Public Philosophy* (Boston, 1955), 46. See also Hans J. Morgenthau: "The kind of thinking required for the successful conduct of foreign policy must at times be diametrically opposed to the kind of considerations by which the masses and their representatives are likely to be moved." *In Defense of the National Interest* (New York, 1951), 223.

5. A. D. Lindsay, *The Modern Democratic State*, I (New York, 1947), 272-74.

6. An intimate and authoritative observer of American policy has stated: "Most foreign policy, in any case, cannot await the initiative of a public outside the governmental executive branch." James L. McCamy, *The Administration of American Foreign Affairs* (New York, 1950), 332.

7. William Y. Elliott, *United States Foreign Policy* (New York, 1952), 25; Richard C. Snyder and Edgar S. Furniss, Jr., *American Foreign Policy* (New York, 1954), 552; Charles B. Marshall, *The Limits of Foreign Policy* (New York, 1954), 13.

8. Henry M. Wriston, *Diplomacy in a Democracy* (New York, 1956), 110.

9. Kenneth Younger, "Public Opinion and Foreign Policy," *British Journal of Sociology,* VI (June, 1955), 169-71.

10. That Roosevelt was less than frank in addressing the electorate in 1940 is attested by his supporter Robert E. Sherwood, *Roosevelt and Hopkins* (New York, 1948), Chapter VIII, as well as by his bitter accuser Charles A. Beard, *President Roosevelt and the Coming of the War, 1941* (New Haven, 1948), 8 and Chapter XVII.

11. One of the most widely quoted reports of public ignorance is by Martin Kriesberg in *Public Opinion and Foreign Policy,* Edited by Lester Markel (New York, 1949), Chapter II.

12. Max Beloff, *Foreign Policy and the Democratic Process* (Baltimore, 1955), 58.

13. Gabriel Almond, *The American People and Foreign Policy* (New York, 1950), 53-86.

14. *Ibid.,* 138-45, 232-33.

15. An interesting discussion of this general subject is that of William A. Scott, "Rationality and Non-rationality of International Attitudes," *Conflict Resolution,* II (March, 1958), 8-16.

16. Lippmann, *op. cit.,* 12, 27, 55.

17. McCamy, *op. cit.,* 336.

18. Daniel S. Cheever and H. Field Haviland, Jr., *American Foreign Policy and the Separation of Powers* (Cambridge, Massachusetts, 1952), 222.

19. For example, Robert A. Dahl, *Congress and Foreign Policy* (New York, 1950), 118-19, 207, 264.

20. Important research on this subject is reflected in H. Field Haviland, Jr., "Foreign Aid and the Policy Process: 1957," *American Political Science Review,* LII (September, 1958), 689-724, and in Roger Hilsman, "Congressional-Executive Relations and the Foreign Policy Consensus," in *Ibid.,* 725-44.

21. George Belknap and Angus Campbell, "Political Party Identification and Attitudes Toward Foreign Policy," *Public Opinion Quarterly,* XV (Winter, 1951-1952), 601-23. Another perspective on foreign policy attitudes is that of Warren E. Miller, "The Socio-Economic Analysis of Political Behavior," *Midwest Journal of Political Science,* II (August, 1958), 239-55.

22. Sir Roger Makins, "The Conduct of Foreign Policy in a Democracy" (Speech of March 7, 1956, Mimeographed by British Information Services).

23. See H. Bradford Westerfield, *Foreign Policy and Party Politics* (New Haven, 1955), 3, 7, 16, 319.

24. *The New York Times* (April 2, 1958), 6. The subsequent paragraphs of the Secretary's remarks are also worth noting: "We operate in terms of an opposition political party, which is

alert and prepared to expose, here at home and for reporting abroad, anything which does not seem to be thoroughly sound.

"We operate in terms of an American public opinion which is highly intelligent and properly critical of its Government—when I say 'critical' I don't mean necessarily antagonistic, but which holds government up to high standards."

25. For an early and important postwar attempt to indicate how the admittedly necessary sacrifices of freedom could be kept to a minimum consistent with national security, see Harold D. Lasswell, *National Security and Individual Freedom* (New York, 1950).